# ELS/Elbasani & Logan Architects

Cover Image:
Strode Eckert Photographic

**Editorial Director USA**
Pierantonio Giacoppo

**Chief Editor of Collection**
Maurizio Vitta

**Publishing Coordinator**
Franca Rottola

**Graphic Design**
Paola Polastri

**Editing**
Martyn J. Anderson

**Colour-separation**
Litofilms Italia, Bergamo

**Printing**
Poligrafiche Bolis, Bergamo

First published September 1998



ISBN 88-7838-040-7

# Cultural Durability
## ELS/Elbasani & Logan Architects

Preface by
*Barry Elbasani*
*Donn Logan*
*Carol Shen*

Introduction by
*Stefano Pavarini*

# Contents

# Preface

*by Barry Elbasani, Donn Logan, Carol Shen*

In 1965, Barry Elbasani, Donn Logan, and Michael Severin completed their Masters of Architecture in Urban Design at Harvard University's Graduate School of Design. Leaving Cambridge, Massachusetts to pursue their professional careers, Severin went to The Architects Collaborative (TAC) who sent him to their office in Greece to design new towns in Saudi Arabia, and Elbasani and Logan went to California to join the planning department of Victor Gruen Associates in Los Angeles. At the Gruen office, Elbasani and Logan participated in the design of a variety of large urban mixed-use projects in Southern California.

On their own, they also entered design competitions and placed as finalists for the design of the Fremont Civic Center (California) and the Birmingham/Jefferson County Civic Center (Alabama).

By mid-l966, Logan had moved to Berkeley to teach at the University of California. In 1967 Elbasani and Severin also relocated to Berkeley. The three former classmates entered a design competition for the Broome County Civic Center in upstate New York. When they won first prize, offices were rented, students were hired, and ELS was born. While the Broome County Arena - the first stage of the successful competition entry and the firm's only commission - was being developed, the three partners continued to enter a variety of other competitions. For young architects interested in civic scale planning and architecture, competitions offered the best, and perhaps only, avenue to implement their ideas.

From the beginning, the firm's interest focused on urbanism. The partners wanted a practice in which the distinction between architecture and urban design was blurred. They thought of urban design as big architecture and conversely, architecture as fragments of a city. By virtue of their training and these interests, the firm sought out projects that would emphasize city living, the most vital form of civilization. These projects involved mixed uses, the shaping of public space, and generating pedestrian activity. Early work included an urban design plan for Yonkers, New York; a new mixed-use commercial center in Kalamazoo, Michigan; a housing estate for 2000 homes in Southern California; and a master plan for Georgetown, Washington DC, which resulted in the design and completion of the first phase, an historic mixed-use center.

The firm attracted clients who were interested in strategic thinking and good design. An enlightened group of clients wanted to "do good" as well as "do well." Clients who were only interested in the "bottom line" went elsewhere. Developers and communities who believed that revitalized downtowns create long-term social and financial return have been responsible for most of the firm's commissions.

Michael Severin left the practice in 1981 to move to London. In 1984, Carol Shen was made a Principal. For the next decade these three (Elbasani, Logan, Shen) oversaw the maturing of the firm. The projects illustrated in this volume represent a cross-section of the firm's work over the last fifteen years - the latter half of the life of the practice to this date. The projects are large and small, public and private; some are cultural or recreational; others are commercial retail and mixed use centers. Two of the projects shown, Long Beach and Honolulu, represent the planning side of the practice, which continues to influence city building at a civic scale. Taken as a whole, the illustrated projects are diverse in appearance and form, responding to different contexts and sponsorship. However, they all exhibit a consistent set of values and attitudes shared by the partners and senior staff of the practice, what can be called *cultural durability*, - plans and buildings that will serve a community's needs for generations.

The designs are a search for responsive urban architecture, one that respects context and the mixture of new and old. The belief is that each city's traditions, culture, and lifestyle contain the seeds for a unique design solution to a new building, the renovation of an older building, or a complex of buildings.

There is a collateral belief that each new structure or place has an influence on subsequent development in the form of a catalytic chain reaction. Thus, it is critical that any design solution, whether for a district, neighborhood, new building or small renovation, be well designed and thoughtfully considered, as it will have an impact beyond itself in ways that cannot be predicted.

The emphasis of the practice is not solely on buildings as isolated objects. Making dynamic urban spaces is equally important. The two are viewed as interdependent. Courtyards, plazas and spaces between buildings - "unprogrammed areas" - command attention in the working method of the firm. Details are no less important than the larger gestures. It is the level of detail, crafted to suit each particular place and specific condition, which makes each project memorable.

Given these values and attitudes, success is achieved if a work builds on the particular traditions of the city, reinforces the surrounding urban context, appeals to its users and the general public, and produces a complementary set of forms and public spaces that are compelling and enduring for their scale, details, colors and textures.

With the globalization of trade and of American culture, there have been increased opportunities to work internationally. The firm has approached its commissions abroad with caution, careful not to violate the idea of cultural durability.

There have been some foreign assignments where ELS' philosophy fits the clients' needs. In Singapore and Turkey, commissions involved renovating and expanding historic buildings for new commercial uses. These collaborations have been successful because the clients possessed a strong desire to knit their projects into the existing fabric of the community.

The practice continues to be invigorated by the inclusion of new voices and talents. In 1992, as the firm expanded, Frank Fuller and David Petta were made Principals. In 1997, ELS added Bruce Bullman, Avery Taylor Moore and Kurt Schindler as Principals. The elevation of these long time colleagues represents not only the growth and success of the firm, but also their enduring design accomplishments interpreting the shared value system. As the practice evolves, the influence of these key players and core staff will continue to grow.

The work in this volume represents only a portion of the firm's efforts over the past thirty years. We appreciate the many architects and designers who collaborated on all the firm's projects, including commissions not illustrated here. (Please sea List of Works and People at the end of this volume.) Collaboration has strengthened the shared values that underlie ELS' design philosophy.

Together, we will create more responsive architecture and plans for towns and cities.

# Introduction

*by Stefano Pavarini*

European observers often have a rather distorted view of American architecture due to a series of clichés in our readings of certain phenomena. We are referring to a certain tendency to pigeonhole into stylistic categories or ideological stances rather than use our senses to interpret things more correctly. Too much rational thinking and, perhaps, an over-emphasis on formal trends and too much history of architecture, literally put the blinkers on us and deprive us of that sense of awe and wonder that only real architecture can stir up in our emotions. Sometimes, as in our case, we need to first analyze the underlying philosophy and technique before examining the forms through which they are expressed. I am actually anticipating the conclusion: for ELS this is more an idea of architecture than a stylistic vocabulary. Architecture that examines the question of longevity, architecture as a means of communicating cultural values designed to raise standards of living. ELS are typically American architects who, however, still retain a distinctly European sense of culture and history, which is seen as a form of critical progression rather than formalistic acceptance of the past, a desire to take action rather than a feeling of nostalgia. They embody American culture's ability to approach history with great attention, but without falling into its clutches like many European architects who get lost in the labyrinths of the past and the poetics of memory and nostalgia; certain American architects show a great capacity to read the fabrics of the city and the historical folds they contain, confronting the past with the greatest possible sense of freedom. This is the humble lesson Venturi's *Learning from Las Vegas* gave us at the beginning of the postmodern era, a period that eventually drew to a disappointing close but whose roots lay in a healthy willingness to come to terms with even the most frivolous aspects of urban life, without the slightest prejudice against even the worst of kitsch as just another form of life. On the other hand, the rather excessive simplifications of European architects inevitably result in one of the following state of affairs: they either end up reproposing the same old stale historicism, including the full repertory of papermache urban designs or Bernini-style propaganda machines, as if we were not on the threshold of a new millennium, or they opt for deconstruction, the super-Modern or whatever you call all those crafty forms entailing a total repression of meaning, history and tradition, as everything except nihilism and the non-sense it creates is completely cut off.

Now if culture can be stretched to such agonizing extremes to express the rather disconcerting times in which we live, as we race ahead of history or trail in its wake, then what kind of approach is left for those who want to construct history in our modern-day cities, actually getting involved in certain key urban issues rather than hiding behind academic formalisms?

ELS are concerned with the age-old problem of how to breathe fresh life into the city's recent history, how to inject new fragments of narrative into an old urban scenario. History as a means of constructing something new, not just a series of props for staging the same old urban set designs. Let's take a look at their actual work: even though the project to revitalize downtown Milwaukee looks like some sort of new rendering of a wonderful architectural past, its forms are actually geared to the kind of happiness and light-heartedness associated with modern-day urban living.

The Grand Avenue's majestic forms are not an end in themselves, they are actually designed as a center of gravity drawing new forces into the city. The project is quite literally a catalyst for urban growth.

The Portland Center for the Performing Arts, on the other hand, is a spectacular design bringing together old and new architecture in a stylistic melting pot of conservation and innovation, as an interplay of urban lights projects a real sense of energy and joy. Light plays a key part in these architectural forms. Visibility is like an urban magnet capable of changing the face of architecture from day to night. The Fairfield Center for Creative Arts is yet another catalyst injecting fresh life into the suburbs. Light always creates a sense of freshness and playfulness, actually taking on the guise of a sort of neon tattoo at the Embarcadero Center Cinema in San Francisco, with its flickering front facade.

It is most important to note how these public leisure facilities - theaters and other stages - have turned into crossroads for urban rebirth, places where people can meet together and socialize in new ways. They also provide a boost to real estate development. Theaters and shopping centers are the new squares and market places where people congregate and interact together. You need to be sharp to sense how and why people decide to get together: the technical skill and expertise of these architects have been tested to the limit in creating this new downtown notion of centrality through the construction of individual buildings like Pioneer Place in Portland, where the corner of an urban building block has been transformed into a real landmark standing out visually on the cityscape.

As we analyze ELS's work in the urban environment, we cannot help noting this almost constant yearning for revitalization that seems to be their trademark, speciality or even corporate mission: to convert anonymous places lost in the folds of urban development into fresh opportunities for growth and expansion. A dynamic new approach to revitalizing the urban environment.

ELS have an uncanny knack of breaking into contexts, injecting their own sense of life and light through high-quality designs that bring renewal and rebirth without destroying what is already there. They belong to that category of erudite American architects capable of combining a European sense of history and place with a typically American sense of pragmatism. A crossover of styles and cultures, a healthy concern for "the art of urban construction", out of the eye of the media and well away from the fads of fashion, but offering a vast array of high-quality projects that shows no sign of waning.

Another issue worth examining is the question of design, the use of geometry in the name of stylistic freedom as a means of revitalising the cityscape. There are no stylistic bonds in their carefully controlled manipulation of forms and signs. ELS use design to create a joyful sense of interaction with the environment. Thanks to their total lack of inhibition, they can create a bold array of daring geometric forms: take, for instance, the aerial thrust of the laminated roofs over the pedestrian ways through the Arizona Center in Phoenix or the radiating paths through its garden.

It is also worth pointing out the carefully gauged orthogonal grid of the University of California Sports Center in Berkeley, a rarefied landmark literally embracing the sunlight.

Then there is the renovation project for the Rotunda Wing of the Mission Inn project in Riverside, California. The original design has been reinjected with a headspinning sense of exotic vertigo through a historical work of architecture penetrated by the sun and invaded by light in a feast of stylistic detail and precision. Let's now return to a more recent design by scrutinizing the playful orthogonal grid with which the Randall Museum Theater is furbished, creating a short-circuit with the undulating design of the audience's seats.

The clever interplay of sunscreens on the Irvington Community Center projects an elegant sense of minimalism.

Basically, there are no rigid linguistic rules or laws, as design is adapted to the problem at hand: old works of architecture are renovated in spectacular fashion, whereas new buildings are constructed around highly up-to-date, rational designs drawing on simple, clear-cut geometric patterns.

ELS are certainly part of that smooth flow of silent constructors responsible for knitting together the built fabric. Analyzing the conditions in which people actually live, they design civic works of architecture involving bonds that are built to last and destined to leave their mark more in people's memories than in fashion magazines. This is what is known as "cultural durability", architecture's desire to make its lasting presence felt in urban life without getting trapped in trends or abstract theorizing.

In this respect ELS's works of architecture are "responsible" for providing practical solutions to the real problems of the communities in which they are built. Their success lies in their popularity with the local inhabitants, their capacity to create life-enhancing spaces by analyzing the surrounding urban conditions and catering for real everyday needs, such as socializing, safety, order and interaction.

They first analyze and then draw out the differences and diversities they actually find, rather than imposing a design created in advance on a computer screen. The idea is to bring out what a place really has to offer, even if it has been left in a state of decay.

It is almost as if the architects were trying to point out that every single part of the city is potentially capable of exercising its own magnetic force, catalyzing energy and conjuring up emotions.

ELS deserve credit for the way they have gradually devised their own intricate approach to architecture that works around the complex dialectical relations between buildings and the surrounding city, new constructions and the old urban fabric, the general background and figurative forms standing out against it, rather than merely trying to simplify matters.

The architect must design his building with the city in which it will stand firmly in mind. He must devise new urban development schemes and strategies which are geared to the buildings they will accommodate. This involves a unified idea of architecture and town-planning working around a combination of different skills and capabilities. Here again the architect has a two-pronged moral responsibility towards his/her art (calling for real competence) and the local community that will judge the finished work.

Their artistic freedom must be geared to this dual responsibility, as they work around the socio-human landscape of forms that already exist or could eventually exist, something only art can extricate from the roots of modern society.

The biggest and most urgent problem revolves around the life and death of huge civil conglomerations. Nowadays, there seems to be something profoundly unpredictable about large-scale urban dilapidation and decay.

In the wake of those great ideological constructs built around the idea of society as a machine, there seems to be a widespread sense of impotency, leaving us at vengeance's mercy as if there were something ineluctably physiological about the metastasis of the city and its parts. On the contrary, ELS's work is shot through with hope and a notion of pragmatism aimed at regaining fragments of truth, pieces of the city that promise better living conditions without trying to change everything. They reject any all-encompassing sense of utopia in favour of the kind of meticulous patience that characterized the work of the old cathedral builders, who were well aware that their work would set an example and be a warning to the community as a whole. The downtown neighborhood of a city is potentially a melting pot of new experiences, as epitomized in the strategic plan for Long Beach, where the site's peculiar features are exalted as part of a flexible development scheme based on cultural events designed to boost the area in the knowledge that injecting fresh life into this downtown district will ultimately be to everybody's benefit. The city is just one entity or rather one single body: if one of its vital organs is infected, the entire organism feels its effects. Each part is interrelated with all the others. ELS's skill and expertise lies in their ability to treat the urban body as a whole, depending on the scale of the project at hand: on one hand, town-planning is geared to interrelations, paths and economic activities firing the kind of growth that can create a busy and varied habitat; on the other, there is the level of individual buildings and their details that draw the attention of and literally captivate even the most distracted passer-by. These architects know how to control the scale of a project to create a self-contained organism, a pulsating fragment of the city made of buildings which are made of architecture which, in turn, is made of details designed around and interacting with individuals. This sequence of interactively cascading elements has a name: design as a means of creating durability and the history of tomorrow.

The city increasingly needs to take hold of lifeless, anonymous spaces, so-called urban "voids". The secret  is to grasp hold of these senseless, functionless voids. We sometimes use the word void to neutralize the explosive potential of dramatic instances of collective discomfort. We end up saying that there are no urban voids, just spaces full of dilapidation and decay! Forms of non-life, destruction and violence sneak into undesigned, uncontrolled and uninhabited spaces. Where there is no planning there is no civilization. We must work on these spaces full of degradation and urban negativity with great patience and precision.

There is no need to try and gain new spaces for architecture, we must simply create a new form of architecture to take the place of its old, obsolete counterpart and this will give a real boost to the entire community.

This is the "niche of excellence" that ELS have rightly attained: a firm that has constructed numerous concrete projects in American cities and is now ready to widen its horizons and expand its interdisciplinary design activities abroad on what is now an increasingly open and dynamic world market.

The global city, resulting from the unification and constant cross-flow of capital, seems to have reduced different cultures and artistic expressions to the same thing, while what really remains is a yearning to belong and some sort of sense of identity for local communities.

ELS's architecture has moved beyond the bounds of America by request of some enlightened clients, using its sense of localism to confront these new cultures free from the bonds of preconceived stylistic schemes. From among all the various examples of their work, we might mention the Clarke Quay project in Singapore, where the entire sense of urban reconstruction along the river banks lies in the delicate balance between old and new, modern technology and a flavour of the past that has been jealously guarded over. The history of the physical contexts in which their projects is grounded is not the only important thing in ELS's work, there is also the important concept of redefining public-private spaces, interaction between open and closed environments, and the smooth weaving and intermingling of urban spatial experiences in the name of continuity, as opposed to rigid divisions dictated by town-planning standards. Everything hinges around the quality of the urban spaces being worked on.

The project for the Kakaako Makai area in Honolulu is a means of creating a new location respecting the local context and empty spaces around it, and safeguarding against indiscriminate urban development. This creates a sort of new "tropical urbanism". If it were not so much of a cliché, we might say that ELS's work listens attentively to the *genius loci* and, at the same time, strives to invent its own *genius loci*. In other words, it looks back towards the past as it projects into the future.

Contemporary architecture must not lose its bonds with the history of the Modern Movement, as an architectural style that deserves to be revitalized: take, for example, the great care with which fresh life has been injected into the architectural structures of Gustave Eiffel's port warehouses in Izmir, Turkey, another fine example of ELS's international work.

As they set out to make their own contribution to the creation of an updated version of modernity, they showed no signs of suffering from an inferiority complex in face of the master of architectural engineering, who played such a key part in updating the vocabulary of modern architecture.

In the wake of the masters of modernity, the firm is working along interactive lines to improve its skills and broaden its professional horizons in the global cities of modern society.

# Works

# The Grand Avenue

*Client*
Rouse - MIlwaukee, Inc.
Laurin B. Askew, Jr., FAIA - Client Architect
Milwaukee Redevelopment Corporation
Stephen F. Dragos - Client Representative
Redevelopment Authority of the City
of Milwaukee

*Architects*
ELS/Elbasani & Logan Architects

*Engineers*
Graef-Anhalt Schloemer (Structural)
Bert Fredericksen Associates (Mechanical)
Leedy & Petzold, Inc. (Electrical)

*Graphics Consultant*
Sussman/Prejza & Company

*Lighting Consultant*
Valley Lighting

*General Contractor*
Morse/Diesel Inc.

*Photographer*
Eric Oxendorf

*Publications*
"American Shopping Centers", July 1992,
    I.M. Tao
"Interior Pedestrian Places", December 1989
"Progressive Architecture", December 1983
"Architecture", November 1983
"Interiors", April 1983
"The New York Times", October 1, 1982
"APA News", October 1982

*Awards*
1988 Urban Land Institute Award
    of Excellence in Urban Retail
1983 Wisconsin Society of Architects
    Honor Award

The Grand Avenue in downtown Milwaukee imports the best qualities of a regional retail center to an urban setting. A catalyst for the city's revitalization, the project's office, shopping, dining and entertainment facilities integrate several parts of downtown, attracting tourists and residents back into the area. The Grand Avenue was conceived as a means to save a deteriorating city core.

In the late 1970's, only two older department stores, Gimbels and The Boston Store, remained downtown. As joint developers, the City of Milwaukee, the Milwaukee Redevelopment Corporation, and The Rouse Company provided the leadership for the urban renaissance that followed.

The concept for The Grand Avenue integrates the two existing department stores and four historic buildings fronting Milwaukee's traditional shopping street.

A continuous two-level arcade with a three level, central skylit court links Gimbels and The Boston Store, creating the plan diagram of a traditional regional mall.

The scheme required renovating the first two levels of six existing buildings.

Approximately half of the retail space and half of the public arcade involved new construction.

Since this project opened, several new office buildings, a new theater district, and the construction of a Hyatt hotel have further enhanced downtown Milwaukee.

Site plan and, below,
axonometric.

W CLYBOURN ST
W MICHIGAN ST
W WISCONSIN AVE
W WELLS ST
PLANKINTON ST
SECOND ST
THIRD ST
FOURTH ST
FIFTH ST

From bottom up, plans of the ground floor, first floor and second floor. Below, historic photo of the old Plankinton Arcade.

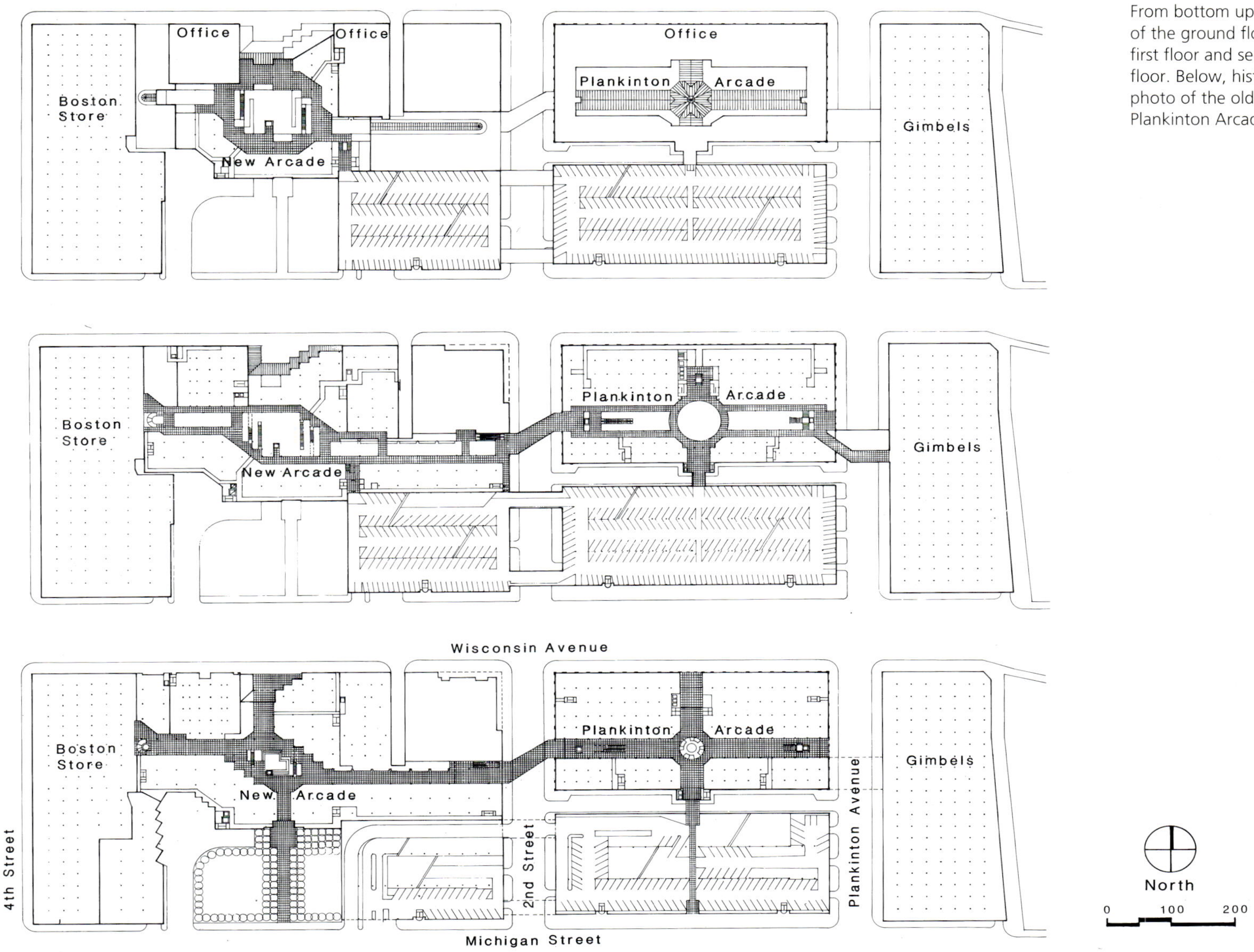

Left, view of new
arcade. Below, view
of the renovated
Plankinton arcade.
Opposite page, the
triple-height historic
central rotunda.

GIMBELS
GIMBELS
Puzzlebox
Deliciously Different
Deliciously Different

**Berkeley, California**
**1983**

*Client*
University of California

*Architects*
ELS/Elbasani & Logan Architects

*Engineers*
T.Y. Lin (Structural)
Bentley Engineering (Mechanical/Electrical)

*Photographers*
Mark Citret
Christopher Irion

*Publications*
"Architecture", March 1990
"Architecture", May 1986
"Architectural Record", September 1985

*Awards*
1990 National AIA Honor Award
1986 AIA, California Council Honor Award
1985 Athletic Business Magazine Facility
    of Merit
1984 AIA, East Bay Chapter Honor Award

# Recreational Sports Facility
# University of California

The Recreational Sports Facility at U.C. Berkeley occupies a compact site at the southwest corner of the densely built campus. Situated tightly within the volume of existing athletic facilities - stadium, gymnasium, aquatics center, baseball field, and track - the project spans existing underground handball courts and new parking.

The complex includes seven indoor courts for basketball, volleyball and racquetball; nine new handball courts; weight lifting, dance and martial arts rooms; and administrative offices. These large spaces are organized around a central skylit atrium and street.

Existing athletic facilities are linked to the Recreational Sports Facility with the new circulation core. The large new atrium was designed to maximize the amount of natural, northern light. The atrium and interior street also serve as a social center, accommodating both formal receptions and informal spontaneous student activities. The facility is not air-conditioned; large louvers encourage natural cross-ventilation.

Existing campus buildings influenced the massing, scale and colors of the project. Three distinct building volumes reduce the impact of the building's large program. Outdoor spaces for students, faculty and the public are provided by the south arcade and plaza. The building defines the edge between campus and community and creates a new gathering place on campus.

Detail of the portico in
front of the main gym.

Details of the exterior cladding on the two separate buildings forming the sports center.

Ground floor plan and, opposite page, view of the main gym.

The corridor separating the main gym from the nine handball courts also connects the new complex to the existing Harmon gymnasium and pool.

# University of California Press

*Client*
University of California Press
The Regents of the University of California

*Architects*
ELS/Elbasani & Logan Architects

*Engineers*
Johnson & Rutigliano (Structural)
Marina Heating & Air Conditioning
   (Mechanical)
BRW Associates (Electrical)

*Lighting Consultant*
Richard Peters

*Energy Consultant*
Sol Arc

*General Contractor*
Christensen & Foster

*Photographers*
Mark Citret
John Sutton

*Publications*
"Architectural Record", July 1989
"L'architettura", June 1989
"Redaktion Baumeister", June 1986
"Progressive Architecture", November 1985
"Progressive Architecture", January 1983

*Awards*
1989 AIA, California Council Design Award
1983 Progressive Architecture Magazine
   Design Citation

ELS prepared several feasibility studies and assisted UC Press with selecting a site for consolidating their administrative offices in one location.

A three story, 1924-era University-owned concrete warehouse was selected for renovation into UC Press' new headquarters. The building now houses graphics, editorial, business and management offices.

The organizing feature for the building renovation is a new central skylight. A hierarchy of public, semi-private and private spaces is organized around a central gathering space. At the core, daylight and low partitions enhance interior spaciousness; full height partitions provide privacy for perimeter offices and conference spaces. The east-west axis at each floor links common functions, such as work areas and conference rooms. The north-south axis links the entry, primary window openings, public spaces and vertical circulation elements.

A recessed arcade at street level and a formal entrance stair link the new street level entry with a second level reception area. Enlarged window openings on the exterior provide daylight and cross ventilation.

A new, formal image was created on the plain warehouse facade with the organization of openings and horizontal striping.

Below, from bottom up,
plans of the first, second
and third floors.


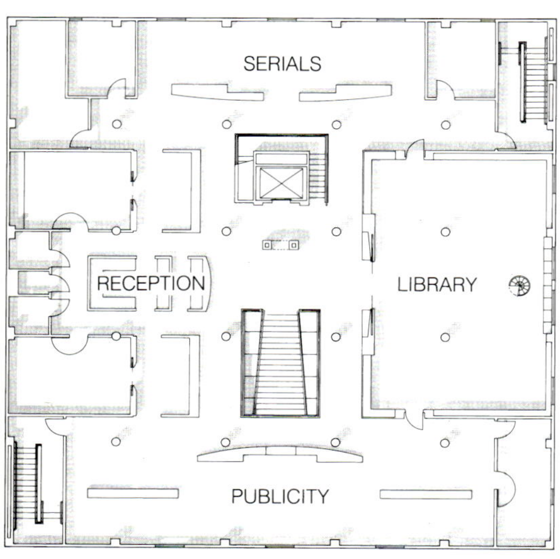

SERIALS
RECEPTION
LIBRARY
PUBLICITY


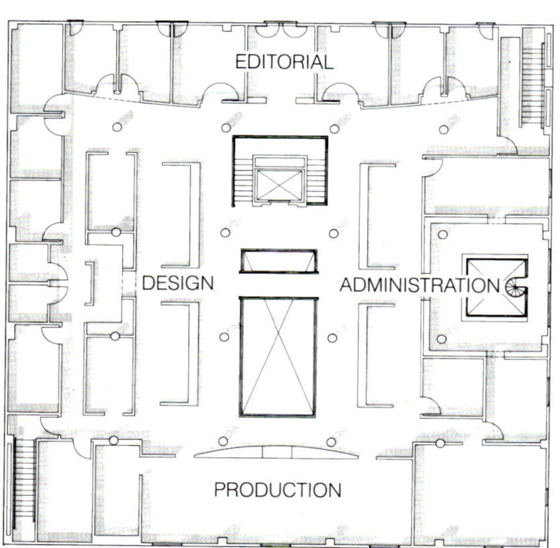

EDITORIAL
DESIGN
ADMINISTRATION
PRODUCTION


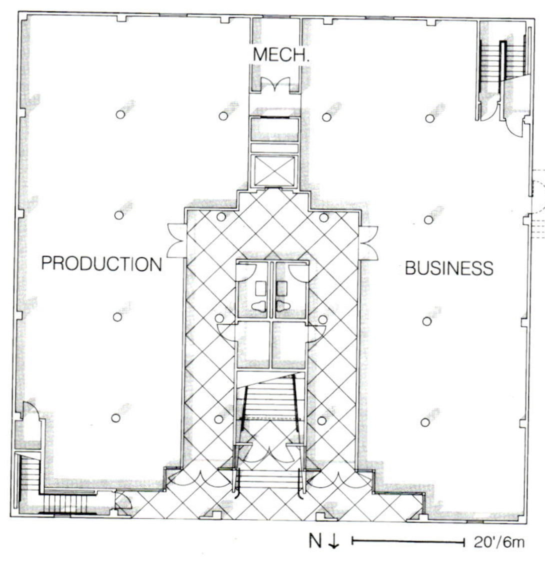

MECH.
PRODUCTION
BUSINESS
N↓        20'/6m

The entrance facade, above, the third floor gallery along the north-south axis joining together the entrance, communal spaces and vertical circulation systems.

# Portland Center for the Performing Arts

*Client*
City of Portland

*Joint Venture Architects*
ELS/Elbasani & Logan Architects

BOORA Architects, Inc.

Barton Myers Associates, Inc.

*Engineers*
CH2M Hill, (Structural)
C.W. Timmer Associates/Syska Hennesy
    (Mechanical)
Interface Engineering Incorporated
    (Electrical)

*Theater Consultant*
Theatre Projects Consultants

*Acoustics Consultant*
R. Lawrence Kirkegaard & Associates

*General Contractor*
Howard S. Wright Construction Co.

*Photographer*
Timothy Hursley

*Publications*
"Time", December 12, 1988
"Progressive Architecture", February 1988
"Progressive Architecture", January 1984
"Architecture California", May/June 1983

*Awards*
1994 United States Institute for Theatre
    Technology Honor Awards
1990 AIA, East Bay Chapter Honor Award
1987 AIA, Portland Chapter Award
    of Excellence (Winningstad
    and Intermediate Theaters)
1984 Progressive Architecture Magazine
    Design Citation
1984 AIA, Portland Chapter Award
    of Excellence (Arlene Schnitzer
    Concert Hall)

The theater complex is located on two adjacent city blocks that front on Broadway on one side and the Park Blocks on the other. The two new theaters share one block with an historic brick church.

Across Main Street, a 1929 movie house and the historic Heathman Hotel are located on the second block.

The Paramount Theater, renamed the Arlene Schnitzer Concert Hall, was a Rococo Revival movie theater and vaudeville house. The design challenge was to accommodate a new, 2750-seat symphony hall, and to provide quality acoustics, structural upgrades and disabled access without compromising the original design. Acoustic improvements were carefully integrated into historic ceilings and walls, and an acoustic shell was added to the stage. Interior ornamentation was recast and replaced. In the lobby, an ornate balcony, in keeping with the building's historic style, was added for disabled access.

Across from the Schnitzer, the new intermediate and experimental theaters share a glazed, multi-level lobby extending the length of Main Street. As theatergoers enter the brightly lit lobby, ringed with balconies, they feel as if they are entering the building on stage. Pediments on the new theaters follow the roof forms of the neighboring historic church. Brick coursing on the new facades aligns with the church cornices.

The 916-seat intermediate theater provides seating at orchestra and balcony levels, in Edwardian style. The 450-seat theater was designed for experimental performances with complete flexibility in stage and seating arrangements. Like the Schnitzer Hall, the new theaters are enhanced by richly colored interiors.

Main Street was repaved in brick reclaimed from the Schnitzer Hall and the new building site.

At sunset, a gate closes off one end of the street, creating a plaza for the evening's events.

PORTLAND
PORTLAND
TEMBO PRODUCTIONS LTD PRESENTS
ROGER WHITTAKER
IN CONCERT NOV 3&4 8PM

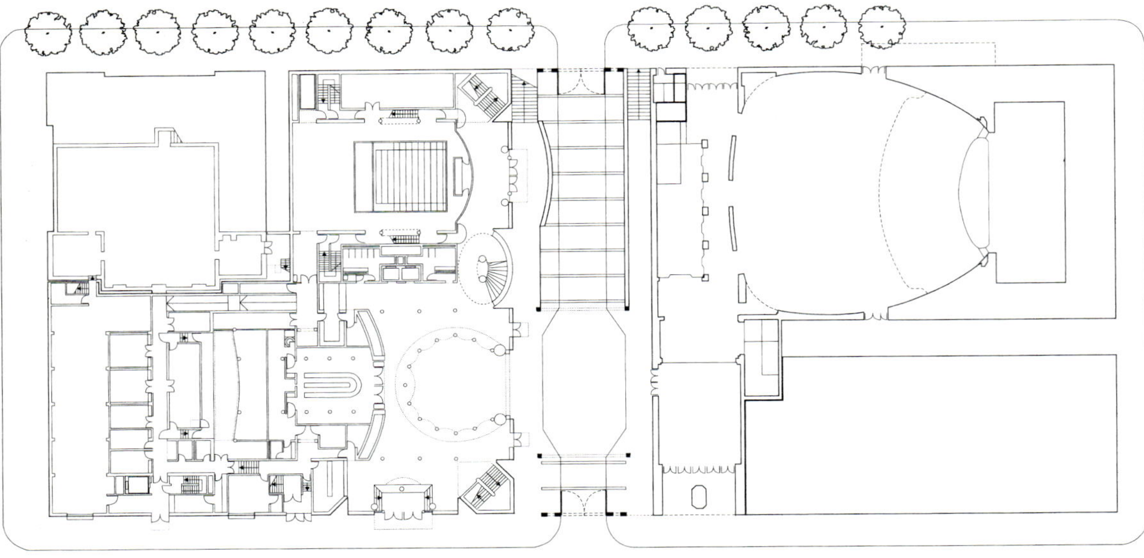

Plan of the ground floor
and, below, view from
the outside of the
theater showing the
large glass wall around
the staircase.

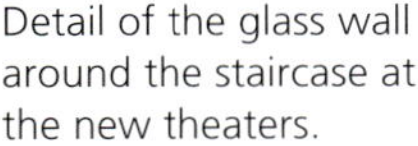

Detail of the glass wall
around the staircase at
the new theaters.

Right, restored
Symphony Hall.
Opposite page, restored
theater lobby looking
towards new theater
complex.

**Fairfield, California**
**1990**

# Fairfield Center for Creative Arts

*Client*
City of Fairfield

*Architects*
ELS/Elbasani & Logan Architects

*Engineers*
Nellie Ingraham Associates (Structural)
JYA Consulting Engineers (Mechanical)
The Engineering Enterprise (Electrical)

*Landscape Architect*
The Planning Collaborative

*General Contractor*
Roebblen Engineering

*Theater Consultant*
Theatre Projects Consultants

*Acoustics Consultant*
Charles M. Salter Associates Inc.

*Photographer*
Timothy Hursley

*Publications*
"Architecture", September 1991

*Awards*
1994 AIA, East Bay Chapter Merit Award
1994 United States Institute for Theatre
	Technology Honor Award
1992 National AIA/NCMA Award

The Fairfield Center for Creative Arts, a cultural complex with a 400-seat theater, art gallery, and meeting rooms, was a catalyst for the revitalization of downtown Fairfield, California.

The City's original theater program called for 200 seats in a converted loft-style building outside Fairfield's downtown. ELS, in concert with the landscape architect re-planning the downtown streetscape, suggested a new theater located in the downtown core would better serve the community. The City changed its course and assembled a downtown site for the new theater.

The light tower at the west end of the building is a beacon that heralds the entrance to the revitalized downtown. New street lamps and furniture (by others) reinforce a sense of place.

The building's long horizontal form on the north houses the loggia and exhibit space, which opens to the street during the day when the theater may be dark.

The arcade element facing West Texas Street creates an articulated wall where a pedestrian or motorist can see through openings to the gallery and the courtyard.

A trellised paseo at the east end of the building connects a rear parking area to the front of the building. Pitched roof forms reflect the local industrial and agrarian building vernacular.

Ground floor plan
and perspective views
of the Center for the Arts
featuring a 400-seat
theater, exhibition gallery
and meeting room for
the local community.


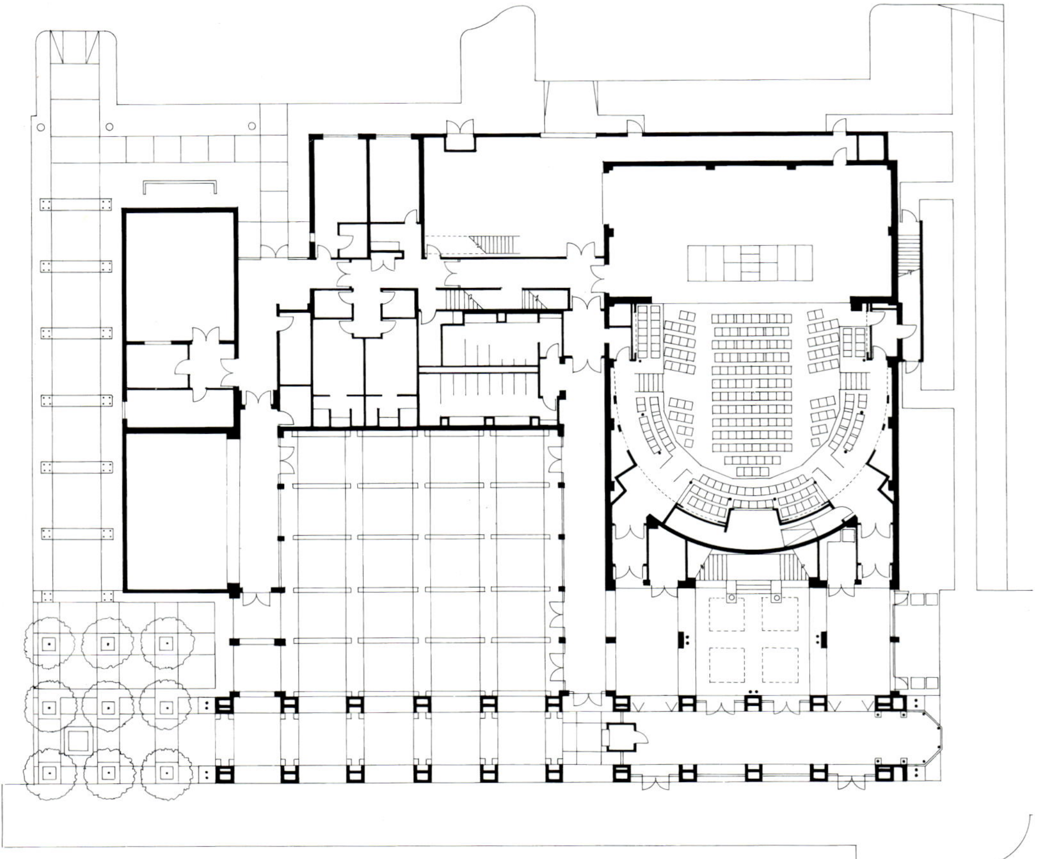

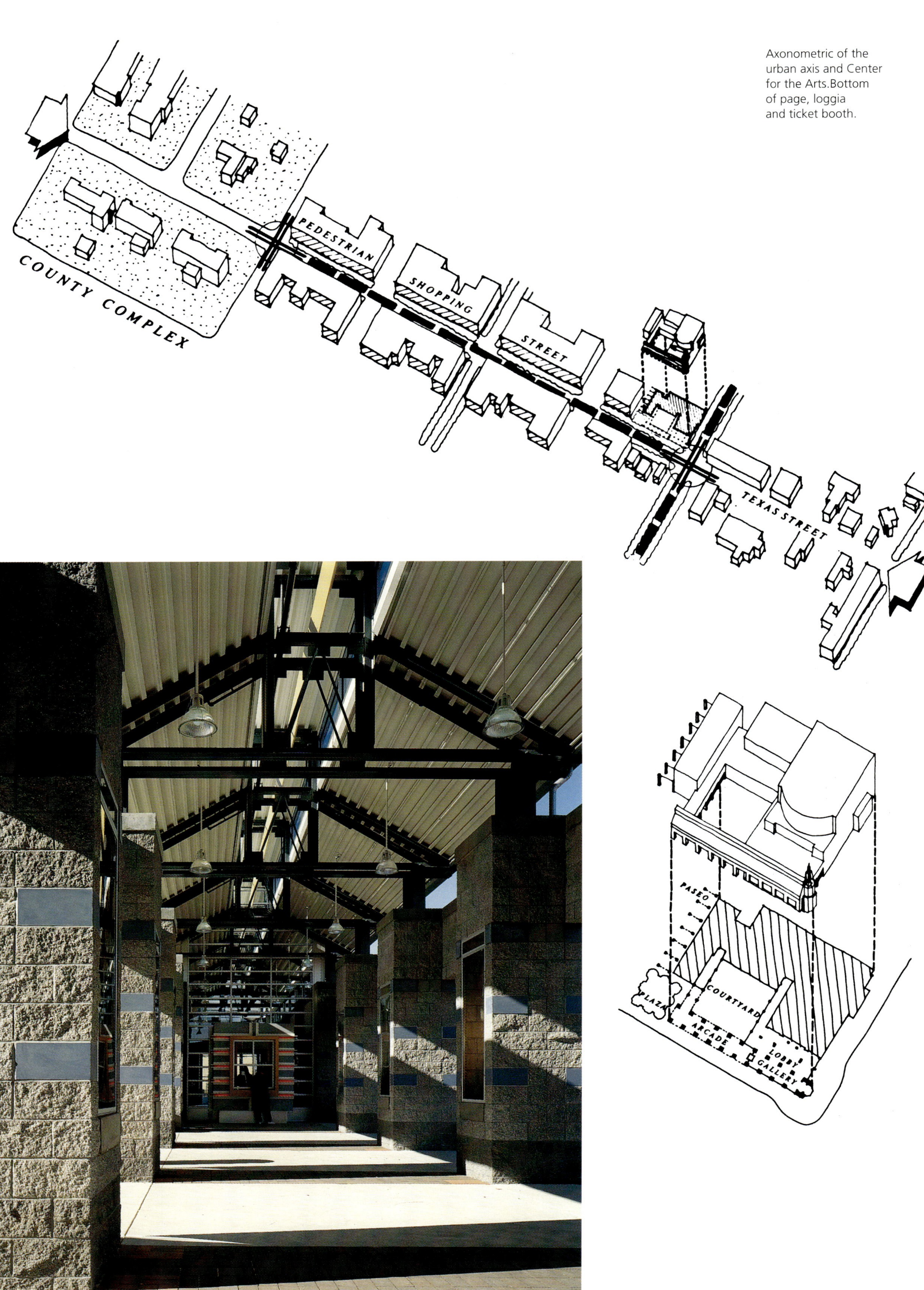


Axonometric of the urban axis and Center for the Arts. Bottom of page, loggia and ticket booth.

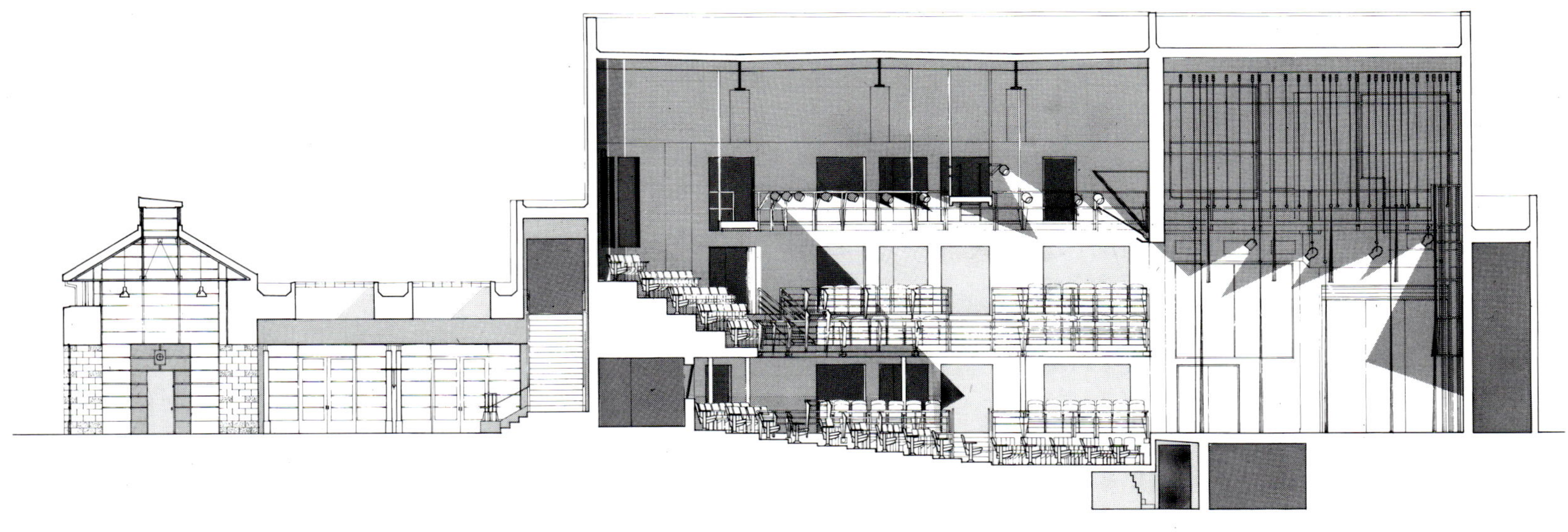

Longitudinal section
across the theater.
Below, the 400-seat
theater.

# Pioneer Place

*Client*
Rouse-Portland, Inc.
Laurin B. Askew, Jr., FAIA - Client Architect

*Architects*
ELS/Elbasani & Logan Architects

*Engineers*
OLMM Structural Design (Structural)
C.W. Timmer Associates, Inc. (Mechanical)
Interface Engineering Inc. (Electrical)

*Lighting Consultant*
Jules Fisher & Paul Marantz, Inc.

*Graphics Consultant*
Sussman/Prejza & Co., Inc.

*General Contractor*
Howard S. Wright Construction Co.

*Photographer*
Timothy Hursley

*Publications*
"Urban Land Institute Proiect Reference File",
     January-March 1995
"Building Design & Construction",
     March 1994
"American Shopping Centers",
     July 1992, I.M. Tao
"The Oregonian", March 30, 1990

*Award*
1994 AIA, East Bay Chapter Merit Award

ELS began working on Portland's retail core as urban design consultants to the Portland Development Commission (PDC) in 1979. Commissioned to analyze development potential for Morrison Street, ELS produced development and design guidelines for four downtown blocks. Subsequently, the City held an architect/developer competition for a three block mixed use project including retail, office, hotel and parking. ELS joined The Rouse Company's team to design the winning submission for the first phase development.

Well below the allowable density, the retail pavilion was designed three stories above grade with an underground Concourse level. The Pavilion Building's scale relates to the historic Pioneer Courthouse across the street. On the adjacent block, the office tower rises above a two-level Saks Fifth Avenue department store at its base and an underground food court, which connects below the street to the Pavilion Building Concourse. Saks is also connected to the Pavilion's third level with a skybridge. Implementation of the third block is now underway.

ELS' design guidelines, prepared for PDC, ensured that the design of Pioneer Place supported Portland's active pedestrian system, with large retail display windows, corner entrances, and glass canopies over the sidewalks. While retail design typically focuses inward and leaves exterior walls blank, Pioneer Place features finely detailed, precast facades with terra cotta trimmed windows at each level. At night, the project is a glowing attraction, with its brightly-lit retail windows. The Pavilion's metal roof and glass skylight complements the cupola on the neighboring Pioneer Courthouse.

The skylight over the central atrium of the Pavilion Building brings daylight to the underground Concourse level. Extending two full blocks below grade, the Concourse connects the Pavilion atrium to the "Cascades" food court. The atrium fountain and food court water features are linked by a meandering "river of light" composed of glass marbles inset into French limestone paving. Bronze and glass light fixtures, mahogany handrails, and well-designed tenant storefronts add to the elegance of the Pavilion interior.

Pioneer Place is a seamless addition to Portland's downtown, its colors, textures and detailing reflecting nearby historic retail and office buildings. Since the project opened in 1990, increased activity has helped revitalize the surrounding retail district, bringing new shops, more visitors, and extended nighttime presence downtown.

WILLIA SONOMA
PIONEER PLACE
PIONEER PLACE
NO TURNS
SW Morris
J.CREW
COMING SOON

The retail pavilion has three stories above grade and an underground concourse level. The scale relates to the historic Pioneer Courthouse across the street.
The office tower rising above the Saks Fifth Avenue department store, is linked to the Pavilion's third level by a skybridge.

WILLIAMS SONOMA
PIONEER PLACE
NO TURNS
ONLY BUS

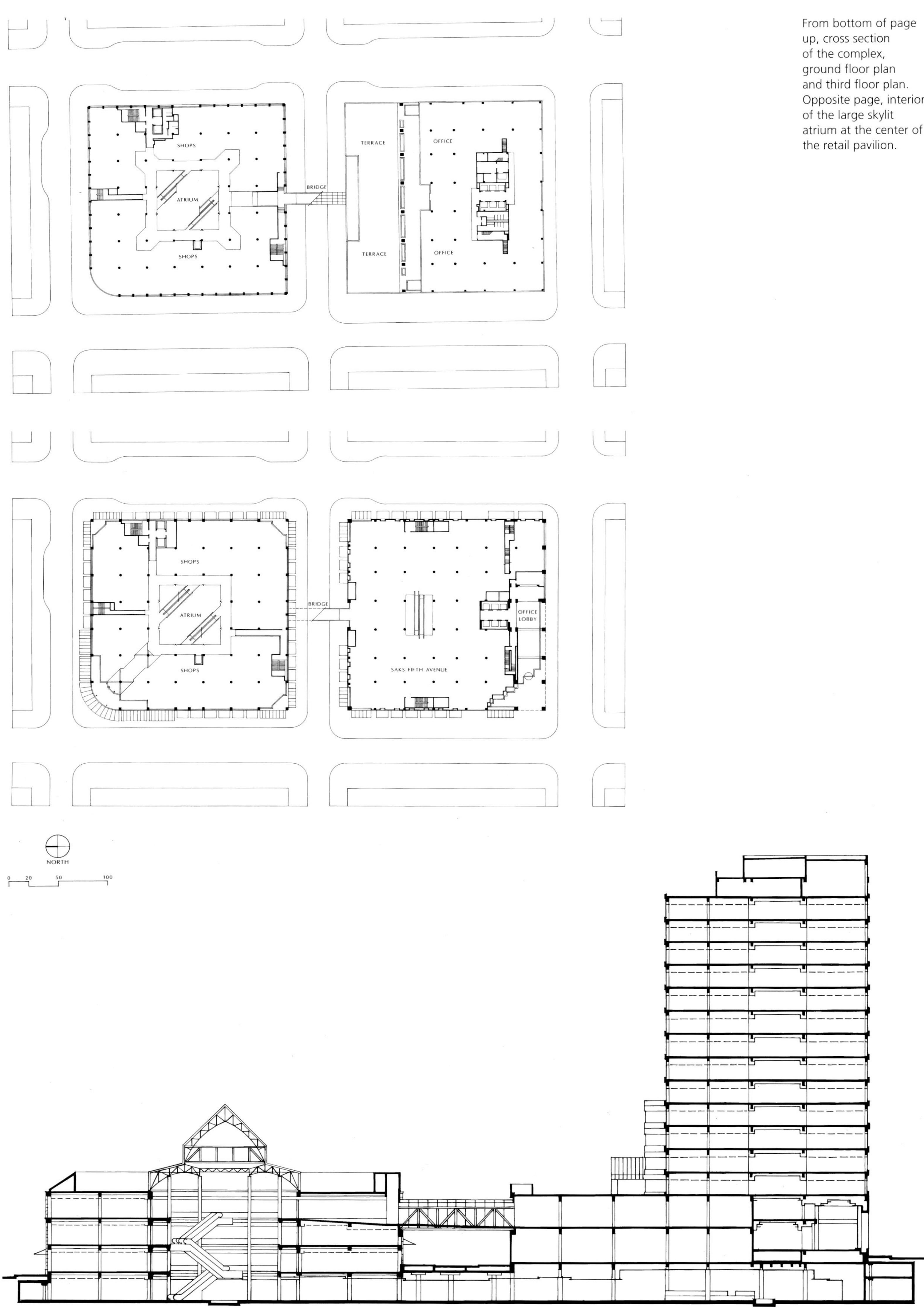



From bottom of page
up, cross section
of the complex,
ground floor plan
and third floor plan.
Opposite page, interior
of the large skylit
atrium at the center of
the retail pavilion.

Nighttime view of the central atrium. Opposite page, entrance to the retail pavilion featuring a curving glass canopy.

# The Shops at Arizona Center

*Client*
Rouse-Arizona Center, Inc.
Laurin B. Askew, Jr., FAIA - Client Architect

*Architects*
ELS/Elbasani & Logan Architects

*Engineer*
Plummer Hasan & Associates (Structural)

*Landscape Architect*
The SWA Group

*Graphics Consultant*
Communication Arts

*Lighting Consultant*
Jules Fisher & Paul Marantz, Inc.

*General Contractor*
Kitchell Contractors of Arizona

*Photographers*
Timothy Hursley
Greg Hursley
Dixi Carrillo

*Publications*
"World Architecture", Special Report, 1995
"Architectural Record Lighting", May 1993
"Process Architecture", No. 103, May 1992
"Urban Land", June 1991
"The Arizona Republic", November 18, 1990

*Awards*
1991 National Association of Industrial
    & Office Parks Best Mixed-Use
    Development

Part of an eight-block master plan for offices, hotel, retail, entertainment, and parking, The Shops at Arizona Center and surrounding gardens provide the focal point for the mixed use complex. The project goal was to bring people back to downtown Phoenix and to create a catalyst for revitalizing the surrounding community.

The 18.5-acre site is shared by two high-rise office towers, a parking structure, cinema complex (under construction) and a lush three-acre oasis (all designed by others). Architectural references, including elements such as the oasis, paseo, courtyard, shaded walkways, and luminarios, respond to the desert climate and Southwestern vernacular.

Retail shops and restaurants are enclosed in three low-scale buildings. Circulation is open air, rather than within an air-conditioned mall. Two linear buildings with shaded arcades form an "L" and align with the downtown street grid. Two levels of shopping and a third level of offices are contained in the "L" buildings, framing the central curved pavilion building. The curved pavilion, a two-level structure of shops and restaurants, features an upper level food court overlooking the central garden.

The control of light, contrast, and shade was a key design determinant throughout the complex. Steel and canopy structures are fabric-covered or open framework at transitions between inside and full sun. Stepped glass roofs protect outdoor escalators, and steel and wood trellises shade the stairs.

Recalling pieces of Native American jewelry, custom light fixtures, stainless steel detailing, and sandstone accents add special touches to the simple building mass. Street walls are solid, warm-toned stucco, while interior paseo and courtyard facades are transparent, shaded storefronts. Arizona sandstone paving integrates garden hardscape, open spaces, and retail circulation throughout the project.

Inviting gardens and shaded walkways, pavilion restaurants on the central oasis, and shops and entertainment have created a memorable day and nighttime destination for residents and visitors to downtown Phoenix.

Site plan and, below,
aerial view of the
shopping complex
and offices.

The food court at the
upper level of the
curved pavilion,
overlooking the central
garden.

Nighttime view of
the two-level curved
pavilion building.

Detail of the shaded
walkway running along
the sides of the central
garden.

Riverside, California
1991

# The Mission Inn

*Clients*
Carley Capital Group
Maureen McAvey - Client Representative

Chemical Bank Real Estate Division

*Owner's Field Representative*
Steve Huffman

*Architects*
ELS/Elbasani & Logan Architects

*Historic Consulting Architect*
Architectural Resources Group

*Engineers*
Johnson & Nielsen Associates (Structural)
JCA Engineers (Mechanical/Electrical)

*Landscape Architect*
EDAW, Inc.

*Interior Design Consultant*
A.T. Heinsbergen

*Lighting Consultant*
Grenald

*General Contractor*
HCC Contractors

*Photographers*
Timothy Hursley
Erich Koyama

*Publications*
Hotel Bars and Lobbies, 1997, Carol Berens
"Hospitality Design", June 1994
"Progressive Architecture", October 1991

*Awards*
1993 AIA, California Council
     Special Merit Award
1993 California Preservation Foundation
     Award for Rehabilitation

The Mission Inn was constructed in four stages with four distinct architectural styles over a period of thirty years from 1903 to 1931. By the 1950's, the hotel was in decline, and in 1985, it was closed.

The hotel occupies one entire block in the heart of downtown Riverside. The renovation of this historic landmark is the cornerstone of the downtown redevelopment. The five-year rehabilitation effort had to meet strict government historic guidelines and was carefully planned to restore the hotel to its original splendor when it was a national tourist attraction and popular weekend resort.

The project involved a three-part program:

1. The Mission Wing, constructed in 1903, needed complete renovation, as it would likely suffer extensive damage in a major seismic event.

2. The three remaining wings required careful restoration of finishes and systems upgrades.

3. The 240 guestrooms and several public spaces needed new furnishings and equipment brought up to current standards.

The Mission Wing was originally constructed of layers of unreinforced brick. The renovation called for several layers of brick to be replaced with reinforced concrete or reinforcing steel rods, and then new plastering to match the original. Unbolted hollow cast iron columns supporting the western façade were replaced with steel columns, anchored firmly to an underground concrete beam running the length of the wing. In the east wing, new steel beams and steel columns were installed within existing stud walls to support sagging corridors and ceiling beams. Mechanical and plumbing are discretely integrated into soffits and chases.

The Seventh Street Arches, patterned after those at Mission San Fernando, were entirely rebuilt. Casts of original ornament were produced to ensure that the new exterior replicates the original.

The Cloister Wing, built in 1910, was influenced by California missions. The Spanish Wing, built during 1913-1914, reflects the owner's extended visit to Spain and resolve to make Riverside a center for Spanish arts. In both these wings, nonbearing walls were reinforced, and unpainted plaster was repaired to match the original. Damaged ornament, such as the finials topping the Spanish buttresses, were cast and replaced with lightweight concrete replicas. The Rotunda Wing, completed in 1931, was influenced by the owner's trip to the Far East. For the restoration of these exterior walls, concrete was mixed to simulate the sixty-year-old patina.

The hotel reopened in 1992 and is once again a thriving resort destination.

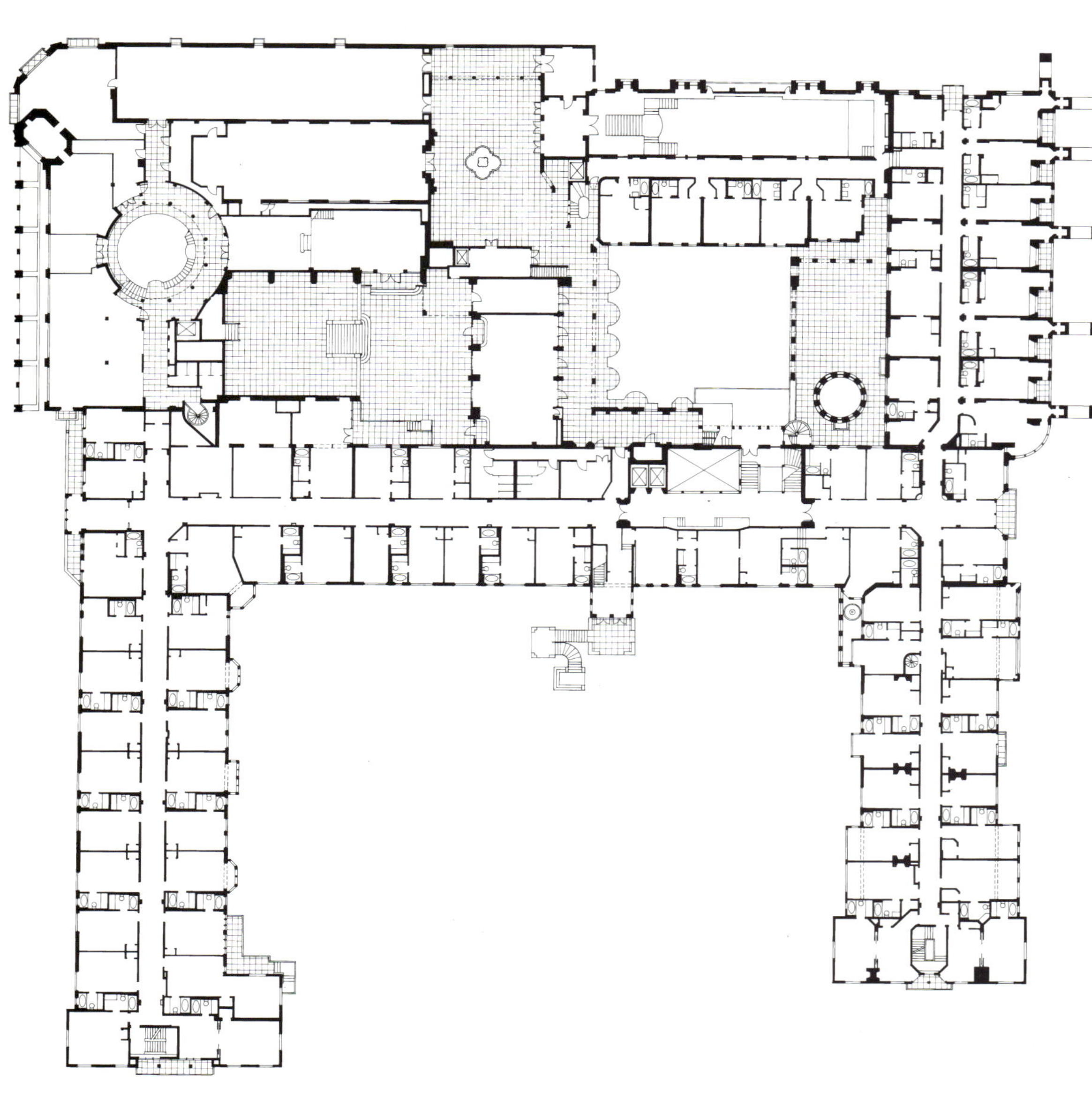

Ground floor plan. Below, aerial view of the hotel. The historic building is part of a redevelopment plan for downtown Riverside.

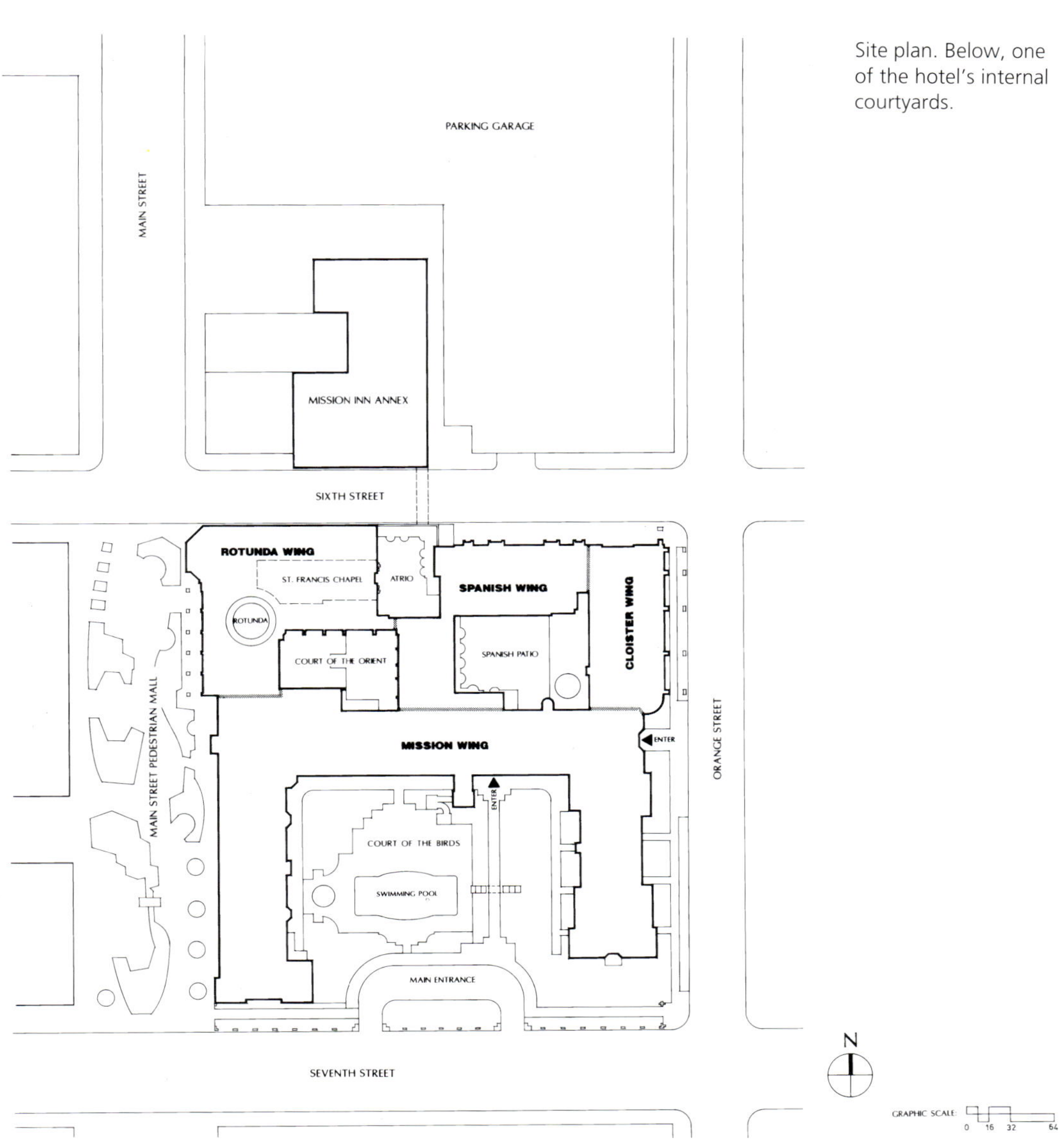

Site plan. Below, one
of the hotel's internal
courtyards.

Views from above and
below of the Rotunda
Wing dating from 1931.
The renovation included
a new concrete
finish that matched
the original.

Long Beach, California
1992

*Client*
City of Long Beach

*Architects*
ELS/Elbasani & Logan Architects

*Economics Consultant*
Keyser Marston Associates, Inc.

*Transportation Consultant*
KAKU Associates

*Graphics Consultant*
Jane Glickman Design

# Downtown Long Beach Strategy for Development

The Strategy for Development is a set of ideas for developing downtown Long Beach over several decades. The strategy includes goals for the future, land uses, near, mid, and long term strategies, guidelines, and a vision for several districts which comprise the downtown. The strategy is designed to change as events change and as the pace of development varies over time.

Working with City government and citizens, ELS developed ten goals for the downtown which focused on making it an important regional destination, by building on its strengths, preserving its unique character, and carefully developing new projects.

Ocean Boulevard is envisioned as an east-west corridor of high-density offices and high-rise residences, designed to capture and preserve views of the waterfront. Pine Avenue and Long Beach Boulevard are emphasized as the north-south mixed-use boulevards, Pine Avenue with a pedestrian orientation and Long Beach Boulevard with a transit orientation. The Promenade area just south of Long Beach Plaza is to be a focus of new retail activity, expanding the downtown towards the waterfront. An area plan is developed for each of the six downtown areas. Area 1, the waterfront, continues as the city's premier location for corporate headquarters, other large-scale office projects, convention-oriented hotels, major civic and cultural facilities, and high-rise high-density

residential projects. Areas 2, 3, 4, and 5 comprise the historic heart of downtown . In the 1960's and 1970's, downtown Long Beach lost much of its retail uses to suburban development. The Strategy calls for the creation of a vibrant, authentic, mixed-use district, which appeals to convention-goers, tourists, residents and downtown workers and builds upon existing retail. Since the first edition of the plan was completed, in 1992, there have been significant increases in retail, dining and entertainment uses, particularly along Pine Avenue. Area 6 represents a potential for mid to long term office and mid to high density residential sites integrated into the West End neighborhood.

The plan prevents sites from being consumed by small, poorly planned developments, not taking advantage of their full market potential.

The Strategy proposes a simple, clear, five-step review process, allowing development teams to minimize risk and maximize design quality at the outset of the development process. Additionally, the Strategy includes comprehensive design guidelines for downtown development.

A few of the guidelines are prescriptive, but most are qualitative, and require judgment. Many of the guidelines reflect general design principles, which are relevant to the entire downtown.

Other guidelines address specific design conditions, which are unique to certain areas.

KRESS
KRESS
FOR SALE
STORE
YOUR LONG BEACH PLACE
First St

This page, diagram
of the main visual axes
and some of the possible
uses for the waterfront
areas. Below, site plan
of the central district.
Opposite page, studies
for possible development
schemes for the central
and waterfront district
of Long Beach.
Preceding page,
revitalized Pine Avenue
at night.


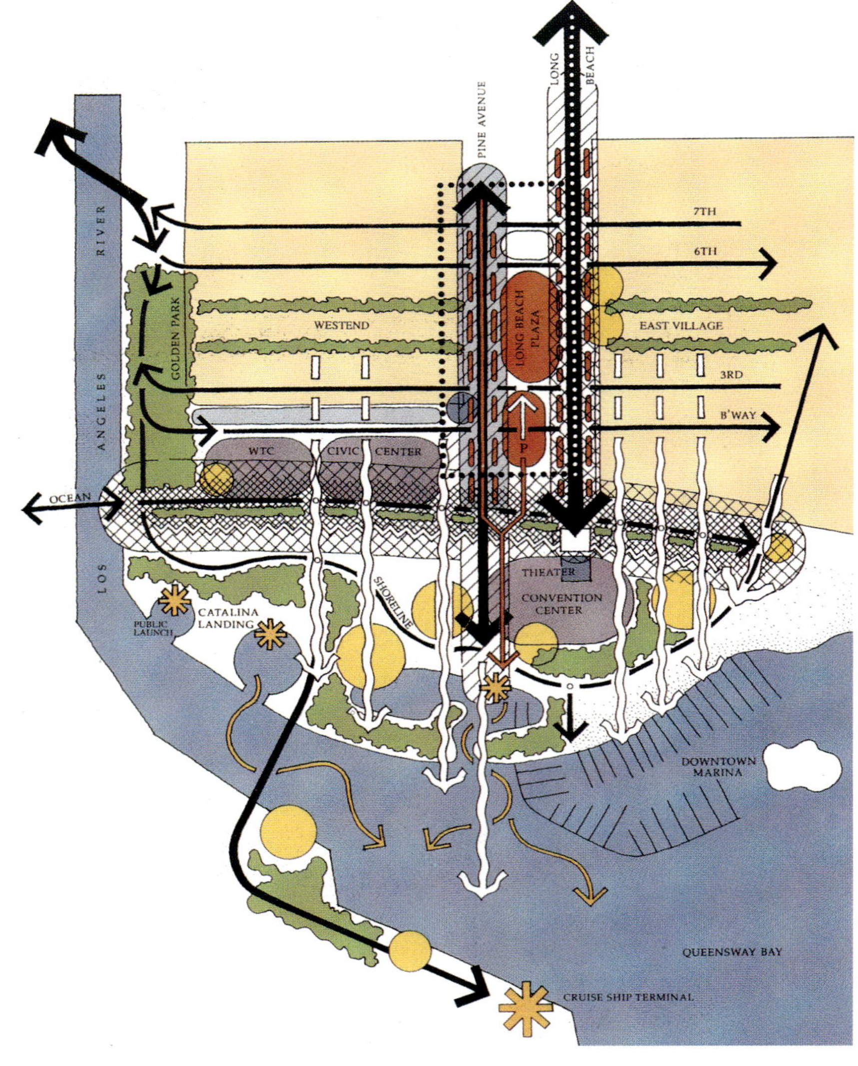

LONG BEACH
PINE AVENUE
LOS ANGELES RIVER
GOLDEN PARK
WESTEND
LONG BEACH PLAZA
EAST VILLAGE
7TH
6TH
3RD
B'WAY
OCEAN
WTC
CIVIC CENTER
P
SHORELINE
CATALINA LANDING
PUBLIC LAUNCH
THEATER
CONVENTION CENTER
DOWNTOWN MARINA
QUEENSWAY BAY
CRUISE SHIP TERMINAL

7th STREET
6th STREET
5th STREET
4th STREET
3rd STREET
BROADWAY
1st STREET
OCEAN BOULEVARD
SHORELINE DRIVE
SEASIDE WAY
GOLDEN SHORE
MARINE AVENUE
MAGNOLIA AVENUE
CHESTNUT AVENUE
CEDAR AVENUE
PACIFIC AVENUE
PINE AVENUE
LONG BEACH BOULEVARD
LINDEN AVENUE
ATLANTIC AVENUE
LIME AVENUE
OLIVE AVENUE
ALAMITOS AVENUE
S PINE AVENUE
I-710

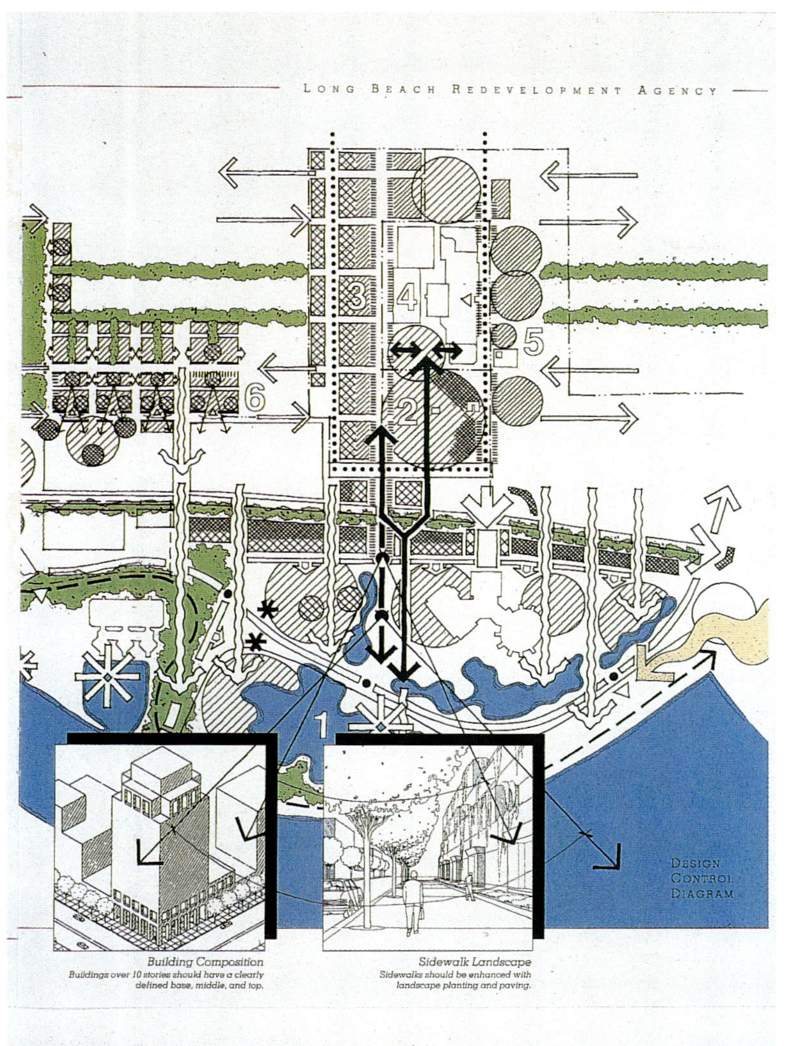

*Building Composition*
*Buildings over 10 stories should have a clearly defined base, middle, and top.*

*Sidewalk Landscape*
*Sidewalks should be enhanced with landscape planting and paving.*

*A vision of Downtown Long Beach circa 2010.*

E L S
ELBASANI & LOGAN ARCHITECTS

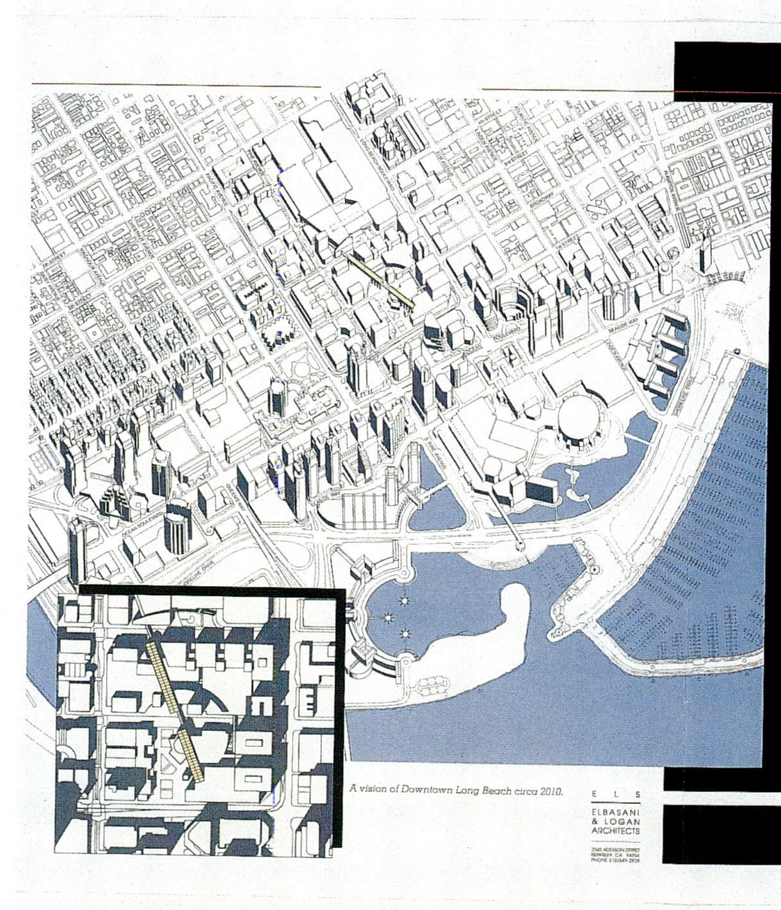

# DESIGN GUIDELINES



## REVIEW PROCESS

**STAGE 1:** **Conceptual Review** occurs at approximately 50% completion of Schematic Design. Projects required to participate in the public arts program should have received approval of their artist selection process and consultants or advisors prior to submittal.

*Submittal received by the Agency, the Agency notifies the Planning Department of project scope and Planning advises the Agency about City policies and applicable procedures.*

**STAGE 2:** **Preliminary Review** requires a complete submittal of Schematic Design materials and the Schematic Design of public art. If the project involves a Disposition and Development Agreement (DDA) with the developer, the approved Schematic Design is included as part of the agreement. If the project requires environmental review, the Agency will exercise authority of certification.

*The Planning Department processes the proposed project through all City approvals, including preliminary environmental review, when applicable. The Planning Department coordinates with the Agency for all City approvals.*

**STAGE 3:** **Final Review** occurs at the end of the Design Development phase, at which time all major design and cost decisions for a project and its public art (if required) should be resolved.

**STAGE 4:** **Design Check** precedes the issuance of building permits. Construction Documents are first received and reviewed by the Agency for conformance with Stage 3 approval. Changes to the documents from Stage 3 are reviewed and, upon approval, the documents are given to the Department of Planning and Building for plan check and issuance of permits. Documents must include necessary provisions for public art.

**STAGE 5:** **Construction Check** and approval of public art is required before a Certificate of Final Completion by the Agency or any Certificate of Occupancy is issued by the City. Change Orders are reviewed and site visits are made by Agency reviewers to ensure conformance with the Stage 4 approvals.

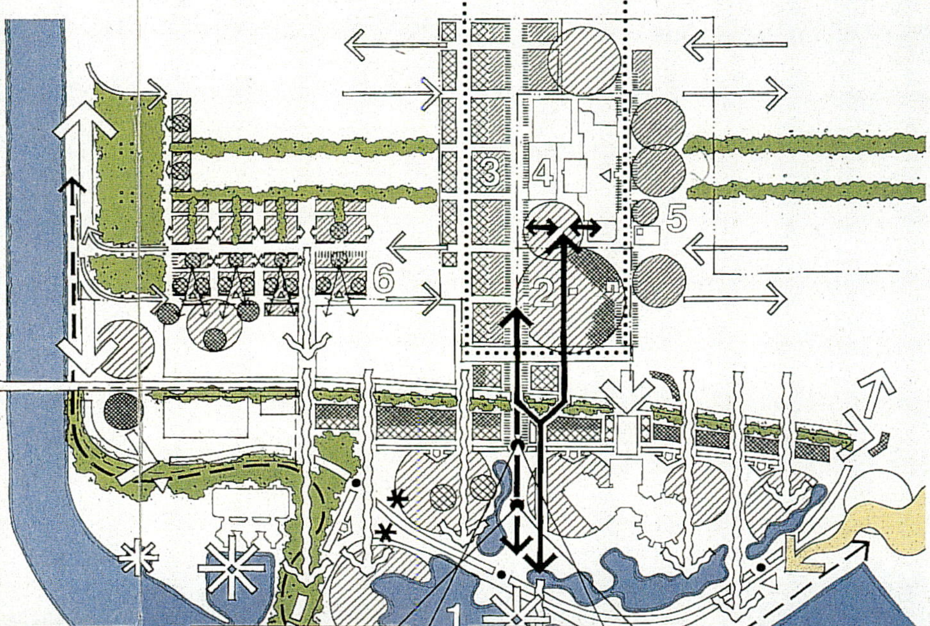

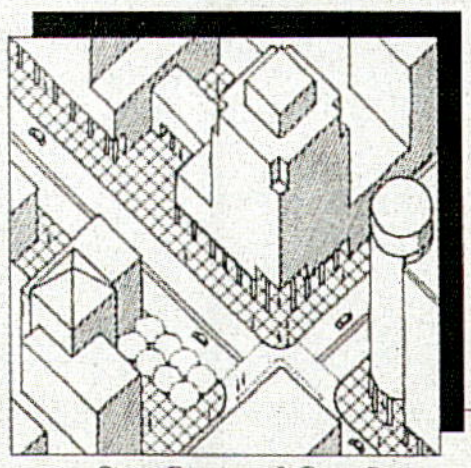

*Street Frontage & Open Space*
*Buildings should be configured to enclose and define open spaces.*

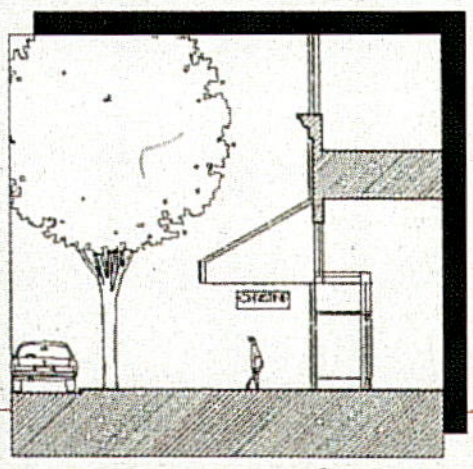

*Storefronts*
*Awnings and signs should respect the architectural integrity of the facade.*

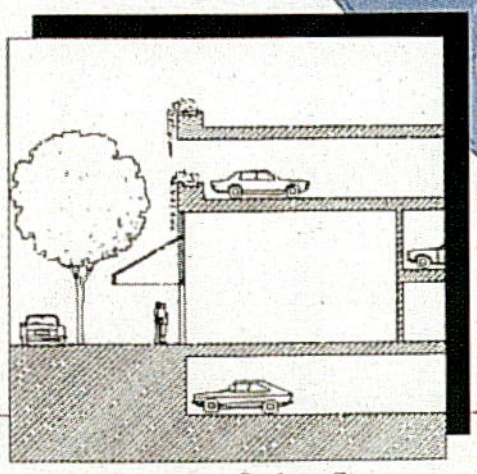

*Parking Structures*
*Structured parking should be screened from public views by architecture and landscaping.*

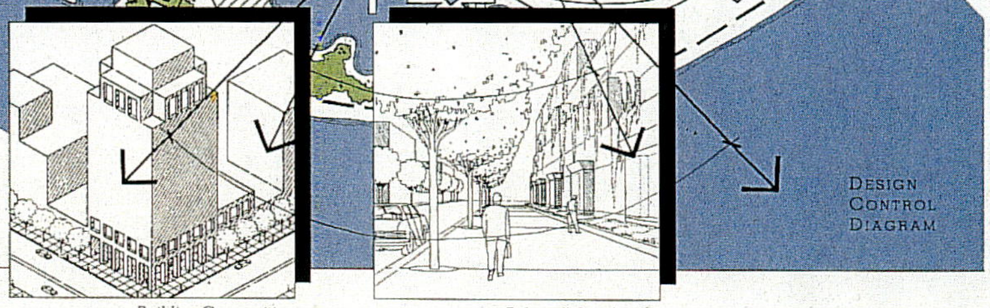

*Building Composition*
*Buildings over 10 stories should have a clearly defined base, middle, and top.*

*Sidewalk Landscape*
*Sidewalks should be enhanced with landscape planting and paving.*

# Clarke Quay Historic District

*Client*
DBS Land/Raffles International Limited
Richard Helfer - Executive Director

*Design Architects*
ELS/Elbasani & Logan Architects

*Local Architect & Engineers*
RSP Architects Planners & Engineers

*Landscape Architect*
EDAW, Inc.

*Lighting Consultant*
Architectural Lighting Design

*Photographers*
Dixi Carrillo
Trends International Ltd.

*Publications*
International Shopping Center Architecture,
    1996
"Architecture California", November 1995
"Process Architecture", No. 120,
    September 1994
"Design Trends", Summer 1994
"Fabrics & Architecture", July/August 1994

*Awards*
1995 International Council of Shopping
    Centers Design Award
1995 Singapore Urban Redevelopment
    Authority Architectural Heritage Award
1994 Asean Tourism Association,
    Best Asean Conservation Effort Award

Clarke Quay is one of Singapore's largest historic renovation projects. Five blocks of abandoned buildings on the Singapore River were adapted and re-used to create a new retail and cultural district. Three new structures were also added.

Singapore was founded as a trading outpost at the crossroads of Asia. The early buildings in Clarke Quay, shophouses (retail with living quarters above) and godowns (warehouses), were built in the 1800's. Tongkangs (barges) filled the river, moving goods to ships anchored at sea.

By 1988, Clarke Quay was abandoned, and several buildings had deteriorated to the point of collapse. Singapore's Urban Redevelopment Authority sought to restore the district because of its historical and cultural importance.

Clarke Quay's architectural heritage reflects cultural influences of European settlers as well as the Chinese shophouse tradition. Common to most buildings is the "five foot way," a covered passageway along the street introduced in 1822 by Sir Stamford Raffles' construction guidelines. These covered walks provide much needed respite from the tropical climate.

The challenge facing ELS was to adapt the old structures to current viable uses without compromising their original character. The design team determined that the facades, roofs, materials, detailing, airwells (enclosed with skylights), and covered walkways were the most significant architectural features.

Some of the buildings were in a serious state of disrepair and required complete reconstruction. Others needed replastering and reinforcement. While the renovation used modern materials and current construction methods, ornament, finishes, materials, and colors were based on precedent. To reinforce the historic character, a broad palette of muted and variegated colors were selected so that the completed project would look restored, but not "new."

A 500 car-parking garage, two new retail structures, and a few infill shophouses were constructed.

Rather than imitating historic designs, articulated plaster facades, timber screens and windows, recessed arcades, and iron gates were used in a contemporary interpretation of the scale and character of neighboring historic buildings.

Within Clarke Quay, the streets are closed to through traffic, creating substantial new public outdoor space for a wide variety of pedestrian activities, including pushcarts, food vendors, and street performers. Along the water, the emphasis is on a variety of dining experiences. The design recalls the riverfront's heyday with broad shaded streets, authentic gas lamps, food stalls and restored tongkangs that now serve as dining pavilions. The local custom of dining out and promenading in the cool evening activates the river's edge, streets, and outdoor spaces at Clarke Quay.

KEY LARGO

The deterioration of the Clarke Quay district before redevelopment. Below, site plan.

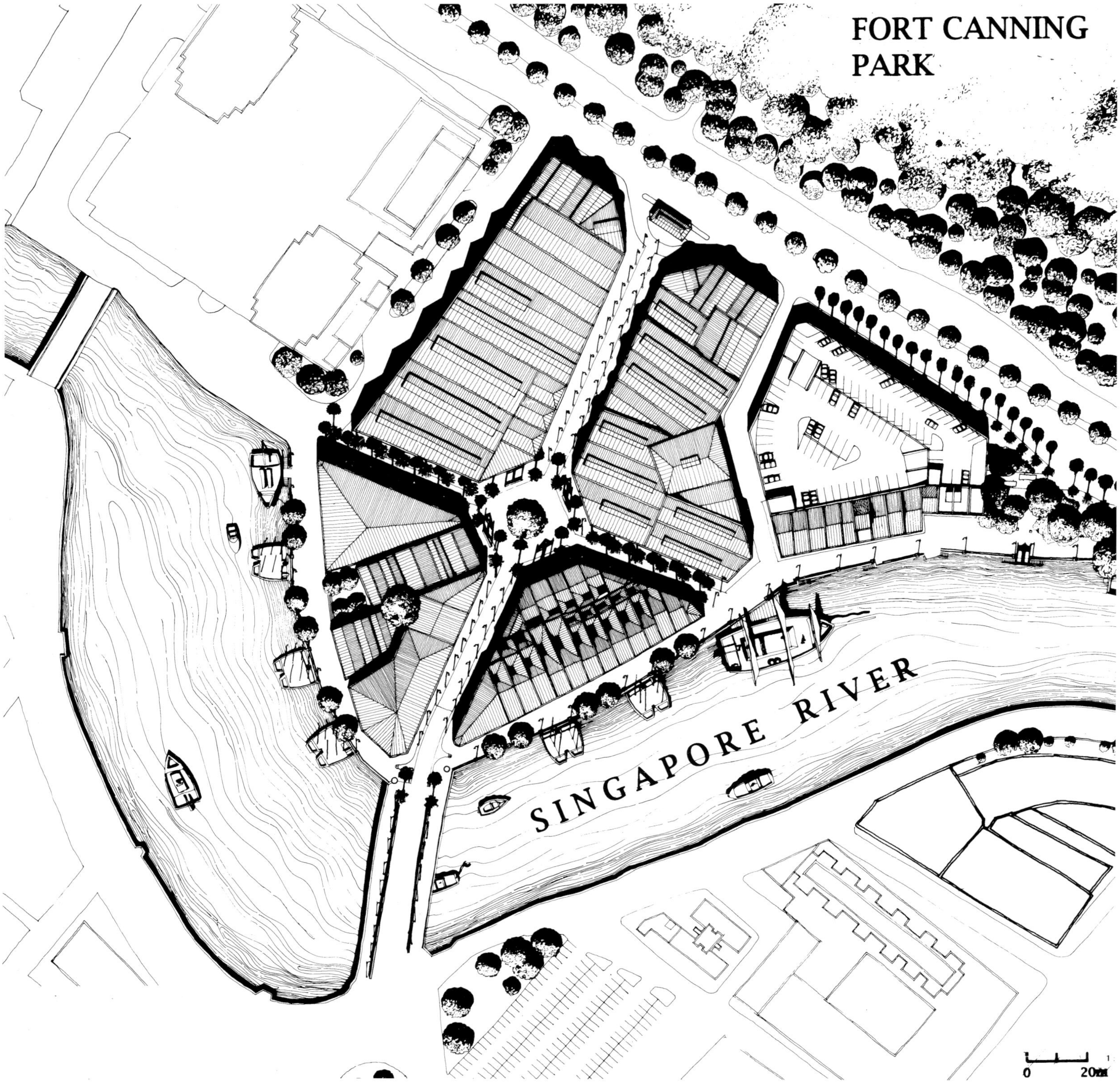

**BLOCK E CAR PARK (NEW STRUCTURE)**
**RIVER VALLEY ROAD - NORTH ELEVATION**



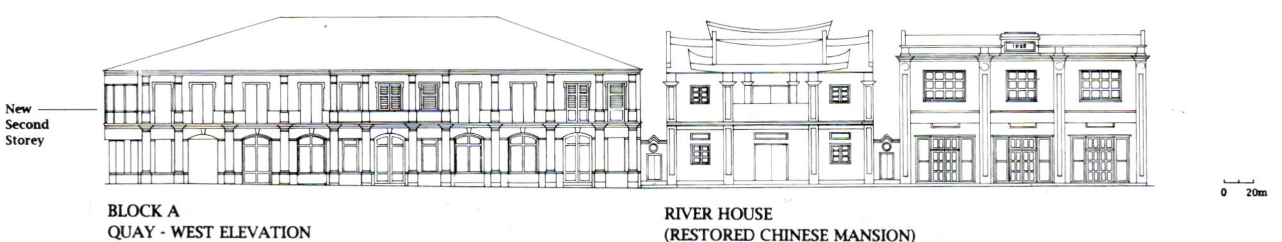



**BLOCK A**
**QUAY - WEST ELEVATION**

**RIVER HOUSE**
**(RESTORED CHINESE MANSION)**

Top of page, north elevation of the new car park and street level arcade. Above, west elevation of three historic building at the river's edge. Below, Read Street, closed to traffic creating a new pedestrian promenade.

Below and opposite
page, nighttime views
of the riverfront. The
local custom of dining
out and promenading
in the cool evening
activates the river's
edge. On the following
pages, Clarke Quay
from the Singapore
River.

# Kakaako Makai Master Plan

*Client*
Hawaii Community Development Authority
Eric Masutomi - Client Representative

*Architects*
ELS/Elbasani & Logan Architects

*Development Consultants*
Stephen F. Dragos
Molinaro Associates, Inc.
The Kalorama Consulting Group

*Planning*
Townscape, Inc.

*Cost Consultant*
Richard Norman & Associates

*Cultural Facilities Consultant*
AMS Planning & Research

*Construction*
Hanscomb Associates, Inc.

*Publications*
"Architectural Record", May 1997
"Hawaii Pacific Architecture", April 1997
"Progressive Architecture", January 1995
"Landscape Architecture", August 1994
"The Honolulu Advertiser", March 22, 1994

*Awards*
1997 National AIA Honor Award
    for Urban Design

The Kakaako Makai Area of Honolulu is a primarily flat, 220-acre peninsula of landfill, with mostly light industrial uses. Just prior to this commission, a major new waterfront park had been completed, and existing plans called for intensive mixed-use development. The goal of the Kakaako Makai Development Strategy was to refine and strengthen existing plans.

Honolulu is not always comfortable with its high-density urban development. Growth is often perceived as "paradise lost," rather than urbanity gained. In response, the existing urban environment has been buffered with wide green setbacks and empty plazas, resulting in a "towers-in-the-park" development pattern. Public activities and street life are declining, and precious rural land is being lost to low-density sprawl at the city's edges. With ongoing population growth, alternatives for development in Honolulu are needed.

The Kakaako Makai Master Plan is a new model for tropical urbanism, one that accommodates increased densities, yet embraces the advantages of a benign climate and informal lifestyle. A clear set of urban design principles were formulated based on the goals of reestablishing the city's links to the waterfront and providing new options for urban living in Honolulu, which combined the best features of city life with the island environment.

The solution superimposes a close-knit urban pattern over a system of interconnected open-air spaces at the ground plane, including courtyards, arcades, passageways, lobbies, and the streets themselves. A rich tropical landscape, as a plan to extend the existing park, pervades the system, providing a unifying element and defining urban character. As the distinction between outdoors and indoors is blurred, the continuous open ground plane becomes the forum for public life as well as a link to nature for Honolulu's city dwellers.

First phase projects, including a 15-acre park expansion, 300,000 square feet of retail, 700-seat theater, 400 units of housing, and 300,000 square feet of office, are scheduled for completion by the end of the century. The entire project build-out is anticipated to take 20-30 years.

# Previous Concept

# ELS Concept

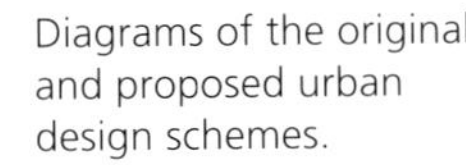

Diagrams of the original and proposed urban design schemes.

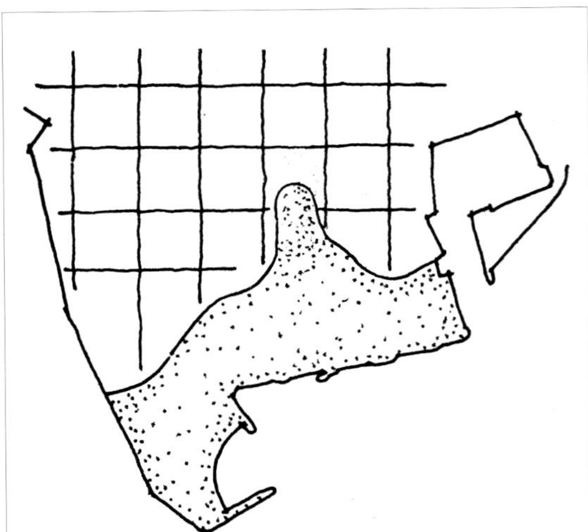

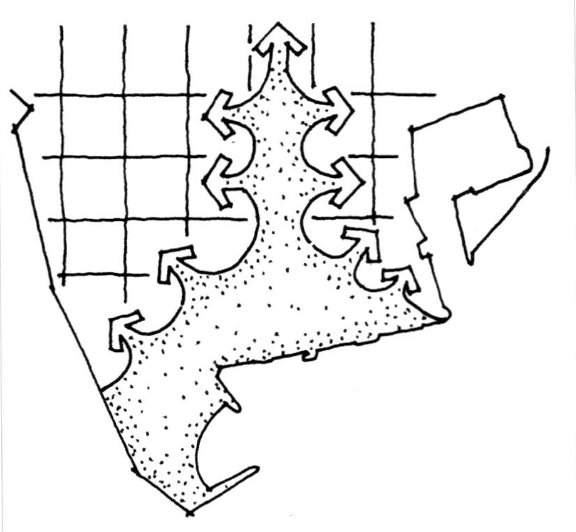

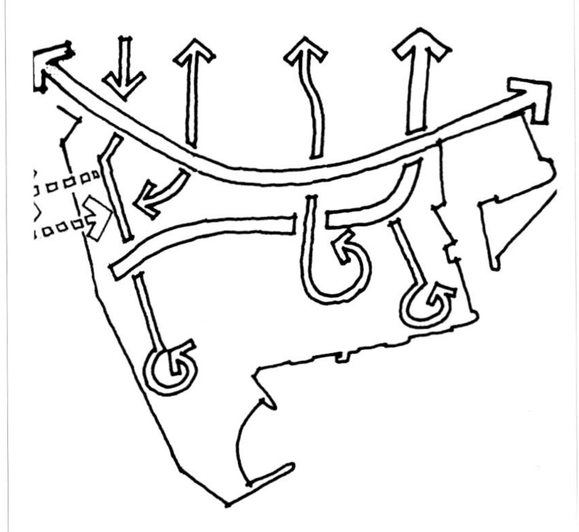

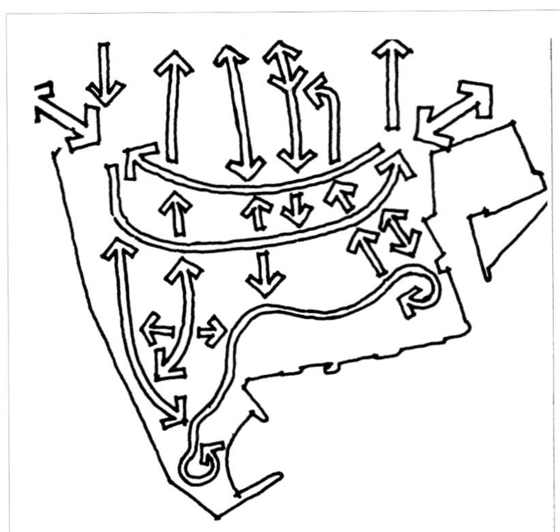

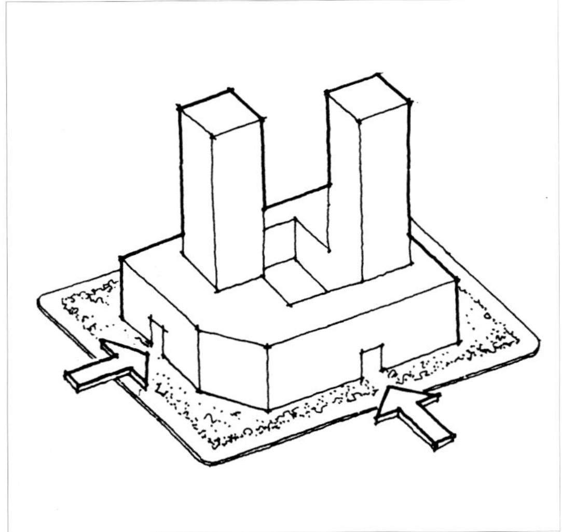

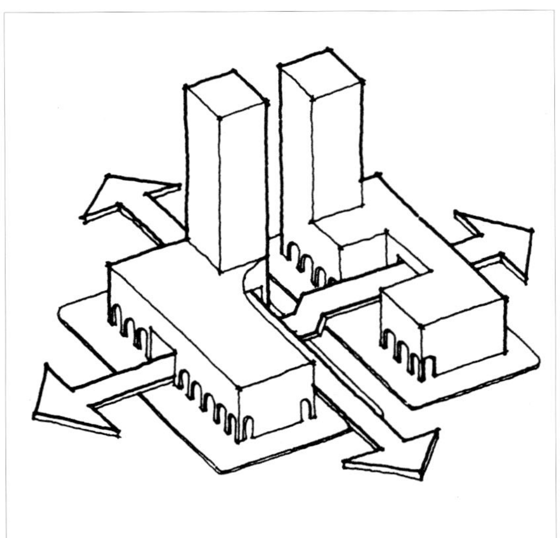

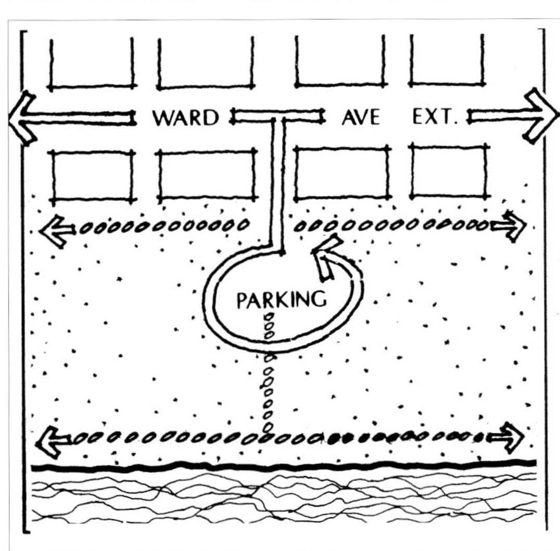


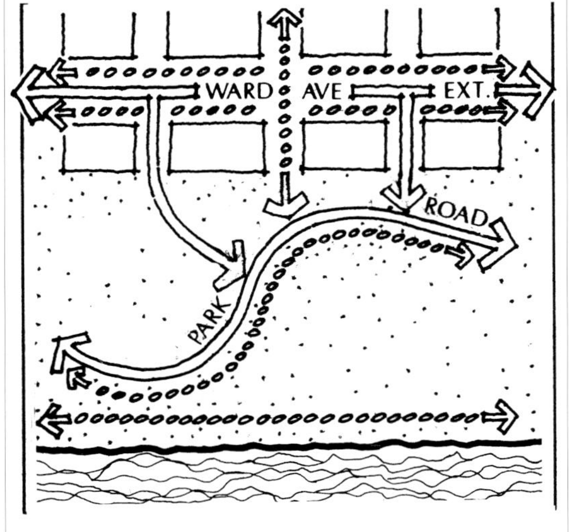

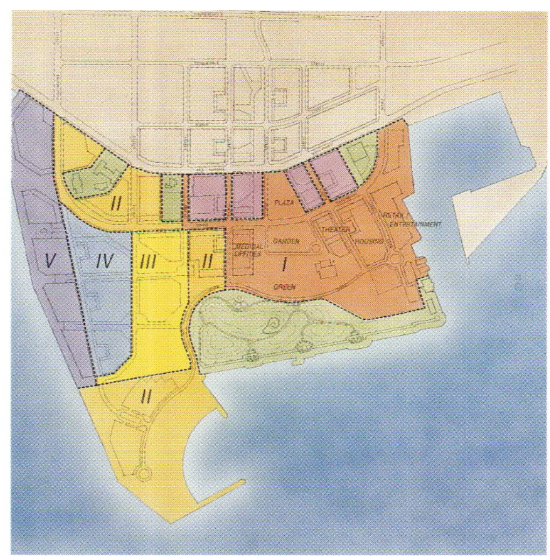

Far left, the phasing plan. Left, illustrative ground floor plan. Below, illustrative ground floor plan of central area.

Central green axis and,
opposite page, park edge.
The project superimposes
a close-knit urban pattern
over a system of
interconnected open-air
spaces.

Alpharetta, Georgia
1993

# North Point Mall

*Client*
Homart Development Co.
Kenneth Jacobs, AIA - Client Architect

*Architects*
ELS/Elbasani & Logan Architects

*Engineers*
L.A. Fuess Partners Incorporated (Structural)
James M. Standard & Associates
    (Mechanical/Electrical)

*General Contractor*
Hardin Construction

*Landscape Architect*
Ashley, Hughes, Good & Associates

*Lighting Consultant*
Luminae Souter Lighting Design

*Photographer*
Timothy Hursley

*Publications*
"World Architecture", Special Report, 1995
"Contract Design", July 1994
"Modern Steel Construction", March 1994
"Shopping Center World", January 1994

*Awards*
1995 International Council of Shopping
    Centers Design Award

The design of North Point Mall looked to the future, while remembering the past. In anticipation of opening just before the 1996 Summer Olympics, the six-block two-level retail center with its nineteen 85-foot steel masts, gleaming white exterior, and vaulted roof with suspension cables, presents a dramatic vision to passing traffic. A continuous clerestory above the roof's parapet brings natural light into the mall during the day, and glows from within at night.

The building's details draw inspiration from 19th century arcades and conservatories. Architectural elements, such as light fixtures, handrails, and floor patterns also recall detailing from last century's building traditions.

Shifting alignments of the main corridors around a series of skylit interior courts varies sightlines within the mall. Glass elevators operate artist-designed counterweights, creating kinetic and colorful moving sculptures. The interior mechanism of the escalators is exposed to view for added visual interest.

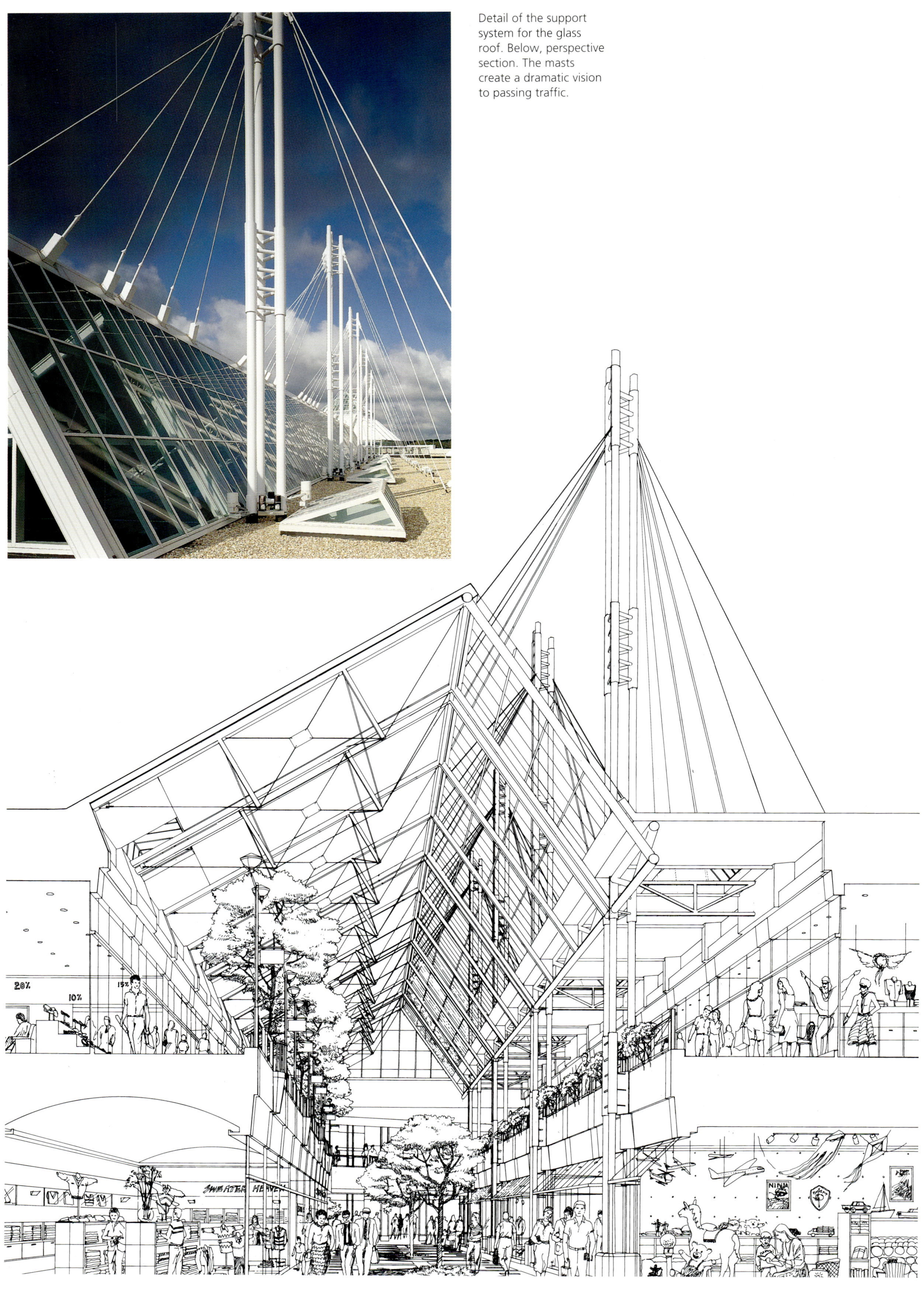

Detail of the support
system for the glass
roof. Below, perspective
section. The masts
create a dramatic vision
to passing traffic.

One of the internal courtyards and, below, one of the refreshment areas. Following pages, nighttime view of the entrance to the shopping center.

# Recreation and Events Center California Polytechnic State University

*Client*
The California State University

*Architects*
ELS/Elbasani & Logan Architects

*Landscape Architect*
Chris Pattillo Landscape Architects

*Engineers*
E.G. Hirsch & Associates (Structural)
Charles & Braun (Mechanical)
Silverman & Light (Electrical)

*Acoustics Consultant*
Charles M. Salter Associates, Inc.

*General Contractor*
Continental Heller

*Photographer*
Timothy Hursley

*Publications*
"Il Nuovo Club", March 1996
"Contract Design", February 1996
"Athletic Business", May 1995
"Progressive Architecture", May 1994
"Progressive Architecture", April 1990

*Awards*
1996 National Intramural-Recreational
     Sports Association Facility of Distinction
     Award
1994 AIA, California Council Honor Award
1994 Athletic Business Magazine
     Facility of Merit
1993 Obispo Beautiful Association
     Award of Commendation

The Recreation & Events Center at California Polytechnic State University at San Luis Obispo creates a new center of social and physical activity and defines the edge of campus.

The Cal Poly setting is rural, yet several infill structures on the campus have resulted in near-urban densities.

At the new Recreation & Events Center, a major outdoor space is configured to conclude two campus pedestrian pathways.

The Center is divided into two vaulted structures connected by a two-story glazed element, forming a three-sided courtyard.

The vaulted roofs recall the form of the existing gymnasium and relate to the vernacular of neighboring agricultural buildings.

The office building, a separate structure, anchors the courtyard and is rotated to align with another campus pedestrian system.

The larger vaulted roof section contains the multi-purpose gym and events center, hosting athletic activities and social functions. A translucent skylight, running along the length of the vault, admits diffused daylight. The smaller vaulted structure contains racquetball courts, offices, and gymnastics rooms. The glazed connection houses locker rooms, weight rooms, and an exercise/dance room. The rotated building contains faculty offices, computer room, and a physical education lab.

The ground floor of the complex is built of cast-in-place concrete and concrete block, which accommodates the sloping site and provides structural shear. The upper levels are framed with exposed steel, which reduces load and cost.

ECREATION
ENTER 43

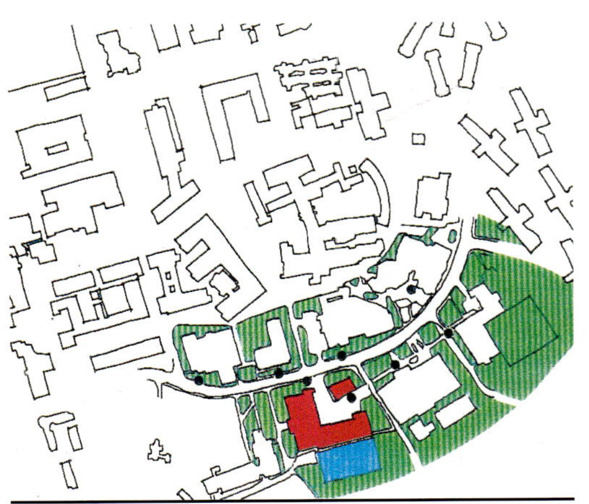

**COMPLETING THE STREET AND CAMPUS EDGE**

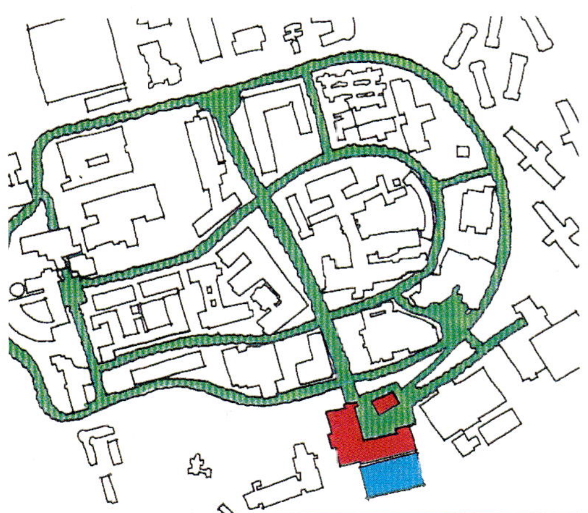

**EXTENDING CAMPUS PEDESTRIAN AND OPEN SPACE SYSTEM**

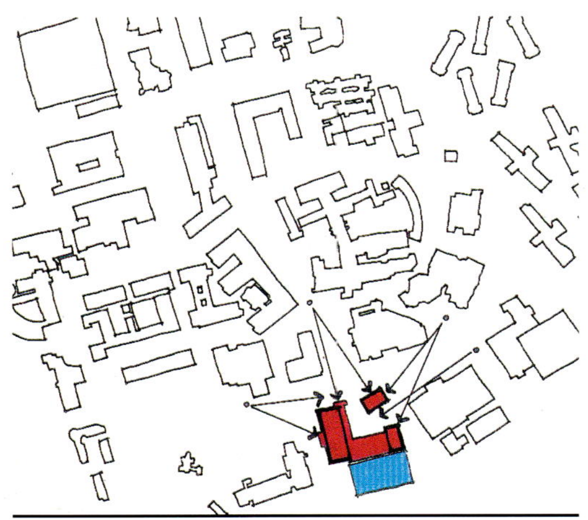

**MULTIPLE VIEW POINTS**

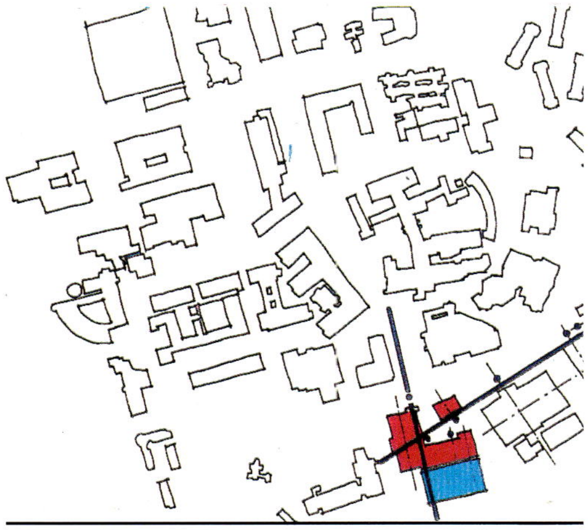

**CAMPUS AXES**

Diagrams for determining building placement within the campus's system of paths and visual axes. Right, detail of the west elevation.

Site plan. Opposite
page, detail of the
north end of the gym
building, featuring
a large vaulted roof.

First-floor plan. Below, ground-floor plan.

Third Floor

Fourth Floor

Basement Level

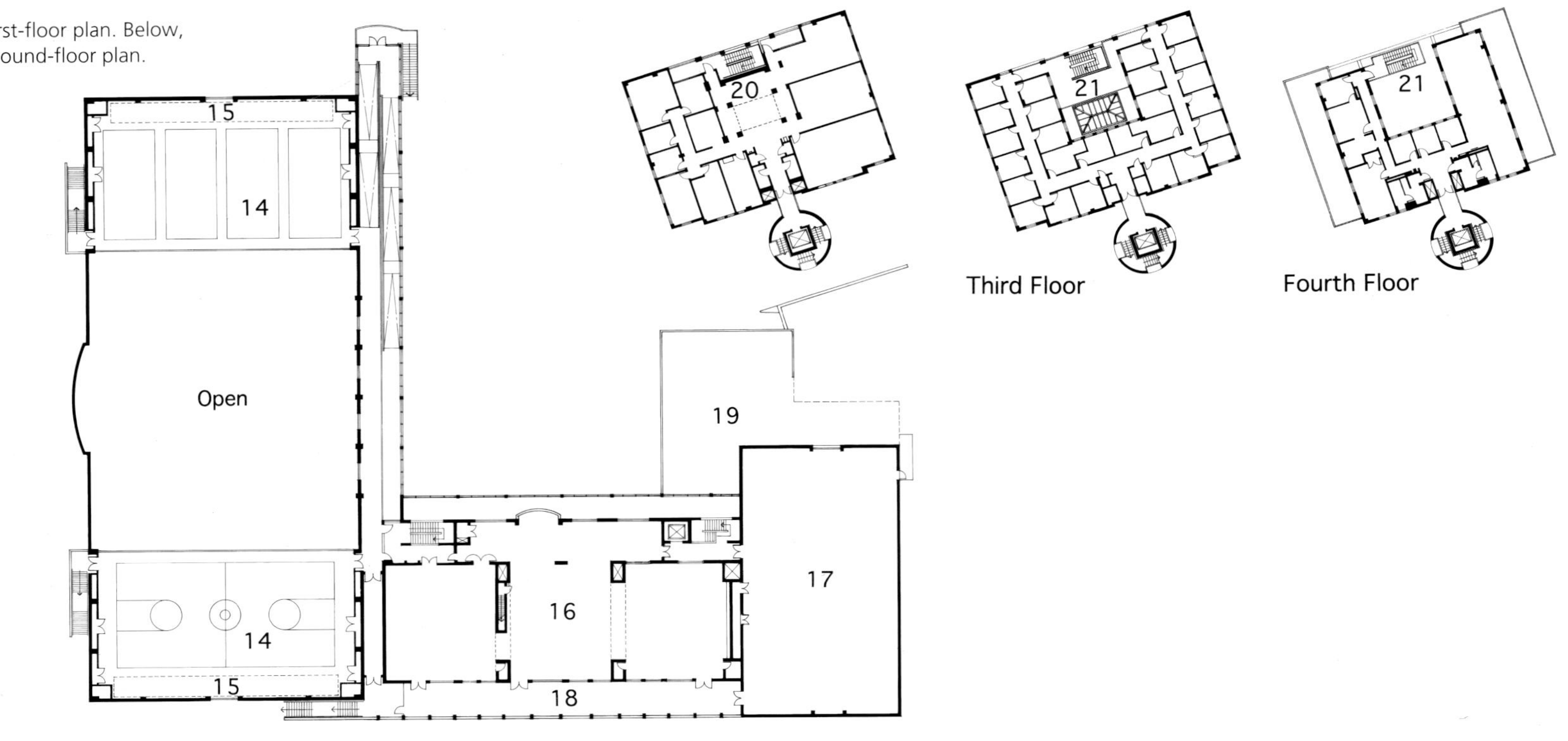

1. Entry
2. Main Gymnasium
3. Retractable Bleachers
4. Wrestling Room
5. Racquetball Courts
6. Recreation Sports Offices
7. Locker Room
8. Dressing Rooms
9. Storage
10. Seating
11. Biomechanics Lab
12. Pool Equipment
13. 50-Meter Pool
14. Upper Gymnasium
15. Retractable Bleachers
16. Weight Rooms
17. Aerobics/Gymnastic Hall
18. Terrace
19. Upper Plaza
20. Biomechanics Lab
21. Physical Education Department

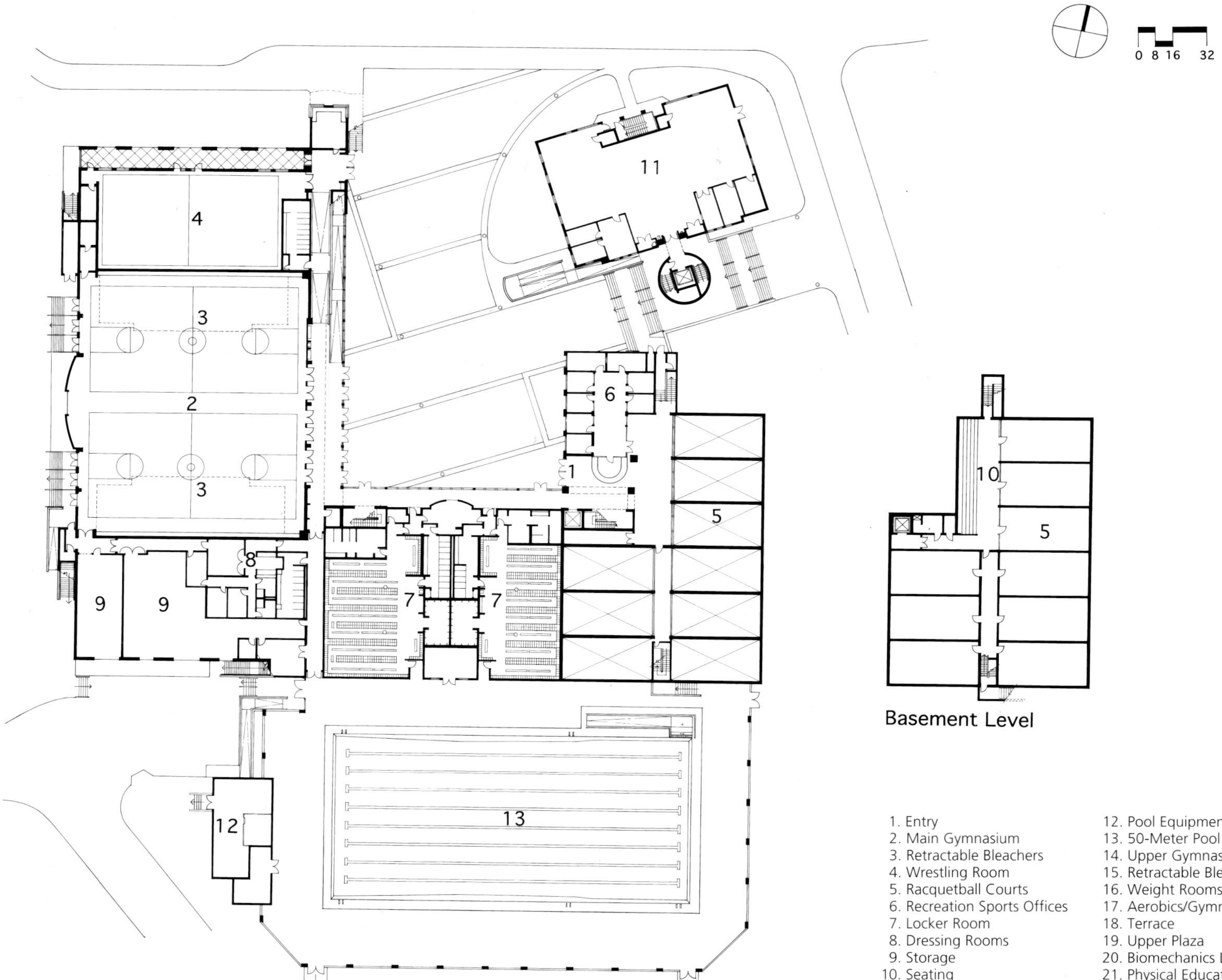

Above, main gym.
Right, interior of the
glass arcade connecting
the various buildings.
Following pages, the
west and south wings,
containing the gyms,
changing rooms, are
joined together by a
glass arcade facing the
internal courtyard.

RECREATION CENTER 43

San Francisco, California
1994

# Randall Museum Theater

*Client*
City of San Francisco
Josephine D. Randall Museum

*Architects*
ELS/Elbasani & Logan Architects
Marcy Li Wong, Architect

*Programming Consultant*
Artsoft Management Services

*Acoustics Consultant*
Charles M. Salter Associates, Inc.

*Engineers*
Tek Pe Engineers (Structural)
Lefler Engineering (Mechanical)
The Engineering Enterprise (Electrical)

*Photographer*
David Wakely

*Publications*
"San Francisco Examiner Magazine",
    March 26, 1995
"Interiors", January 1995
"Interior Design", October 1994

*Awards*
1995 United States Institute for Theatre
    Technology Honor Award
1995 16th Annual Interiors Magazine Award
1994 AIA, San Francisco Chapter Merit Award

Retained by the San Francisco Department of Parks & Recreation, ELS, working with Marcy Li Wong Architect, developed a 25-year master plan for a popular children's museum. The Randall Museum includes a theater, art gallery, and spaces for animal study, crafts, and natural history. The study provided phasing, cost estimates, and financing concepts, and recommended that renovation of the 200-seat auditorium, dressing rooms, and public restrooms be included in the first phase.

The City Public Works Department constructed the museum in 1951. In the new Master Plan, the architects suggested the auditorium, an unadorned concrete shell, be renovated and converted to a live performance theater for children, adolescent, and adult productions. The plan also identified several deficiencies, including poor sight lines, insufficient floor slope and stage depth, an inflexible seating arrangement, lack of theater lighting or rigging, poor acoustics and a noisy mechanical system.

With fixed ceilings and walls, redesign was constrained to the existing auditorium space. The most dramatic modification was constructing a new floor and providing seating at a steep rake.

This change improved sight lines, provided theater flexibility, and added new storage space, a control booth, and a small foyer.

The stage was expanded outward onto the raised floor. Isolating the existing mechanical unit above the stage, introducing a plenum in front of the stage area, and installing sound insulation on the walls and carpeting on the floor and seats improved the acoustics. A grid in front of the stage holds professional theater lighting. Above the seats, at the rear of the theater, a booth for lighting and sound control was added.

The deep purple hue on the walls helps to focus attention towards the stage. New elements, such as the lighting grid, acoustical wall grid, handrails, seating, and control booth, were highlighted in brighter colors. Raked seating was constructed toward the rear of the room. The curving form of the fixed seating complements the design of portable chairs. The chairs are stored underneath the raked seating. In front of the stage, the flat floor can be used for additional seating or small performances. Curves and waves contrast with the angular wood panels and grids, creating a sense of drama and whimsy.

Theater plan. Opposite
page, longitudinal
section and 200-seat
hall.

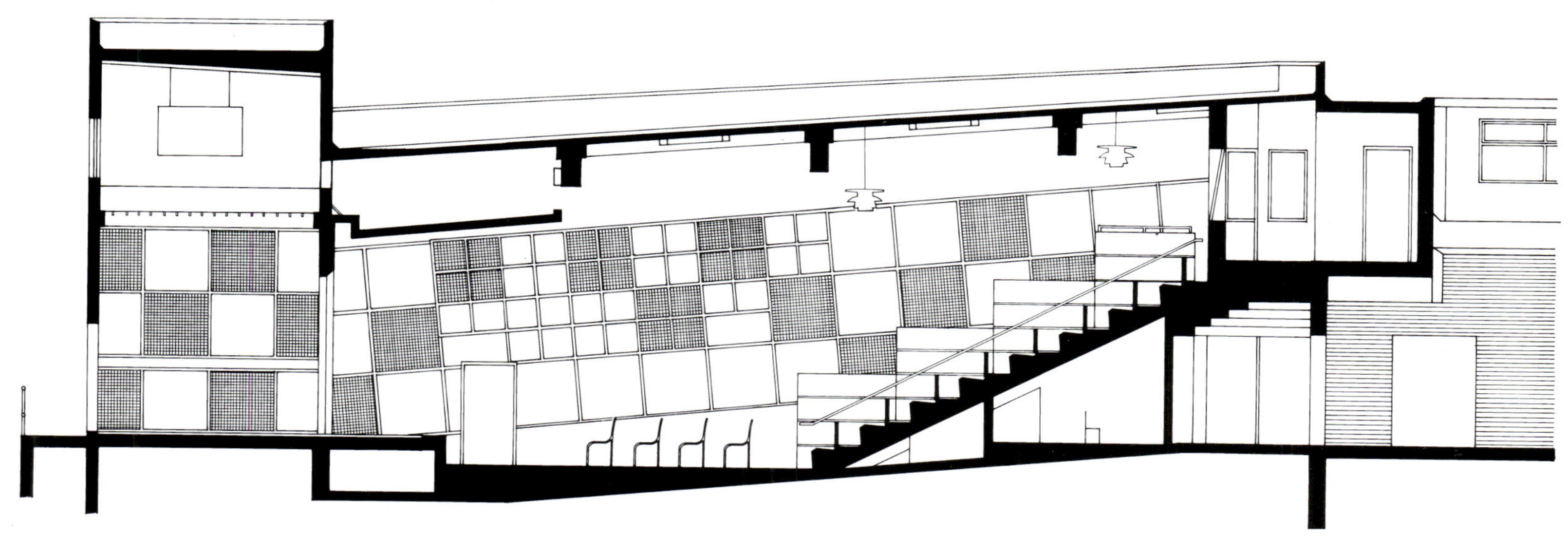

San Francisco, California
1995

# Embarcadero Center Renovation and Cinema Complex

*Clients*
Rockefeller Properties
Prudential Property Company

Pacific Property Services
Herb Lembcke, FAIA - Client Architect

*Architects*
ELS/Elbasani & Logan Architects

*Theater Interiors*
Graham Little Studios

*Engineers*
Dasse Design (Structural)
Glumac Associates (Mechanical/Electrical)

*Lighting Consultant*
Ross DeAlessi Lighting Design

*General Contractor*
Dinwiddie Construction Company

*Graphics Consultants*
Deborah Nichols (Cinema)
Richard Poulin Design Group (Commercial)

*Photographer*
John Sutton

*Publications*
"WIND - World Interior Design", Spring 1997
"Building Design & Construction",
    December 1996
"Architectural Record Lighting",
    November 1996

At the four-block Embarcadero Center complex, one retail building is sited on the north side of an high-rise office tower. Without sunlight or pedestrian activity, the third level of this building had been difficult to lease. The roof over the former retail spaces was raised to accommodate five new cinemas, and existing exterior space was enclosed and renovated into an elegant new lobby.

Cinemas were added to energize the entire Embarcadero Center, particularly in the evenings and on weekends. Located at the edge of the financial district, there was sufficient traffic for retail and restaurant tenants on weekdays, but less activity occurred at other times. The new cinema complex increases evening and weekend pedestrian traffic and attracts patrons to the Center's restaurants. The design of the cinema addition respects the character of the existing complex (originally designed by John Portman & Associates, Inc.) and is carefully integrated into the existing architectural context.

The cinema elevations serve as a "canvas" for new neon graphic elements. The simple building form activated by dramatic night lighting enlivens San Francisco's twenty-year old landmark mixed-use center.

The cinemas were part of a larger renovation, which included improvements and additions to the Embarcadero Center retail and public spaces and to the Hyatt Regency Hotel.

CINEMA

One of the five new movie theaters in the complex. Below, plan of the third level of the complex where the movie theaters are built.

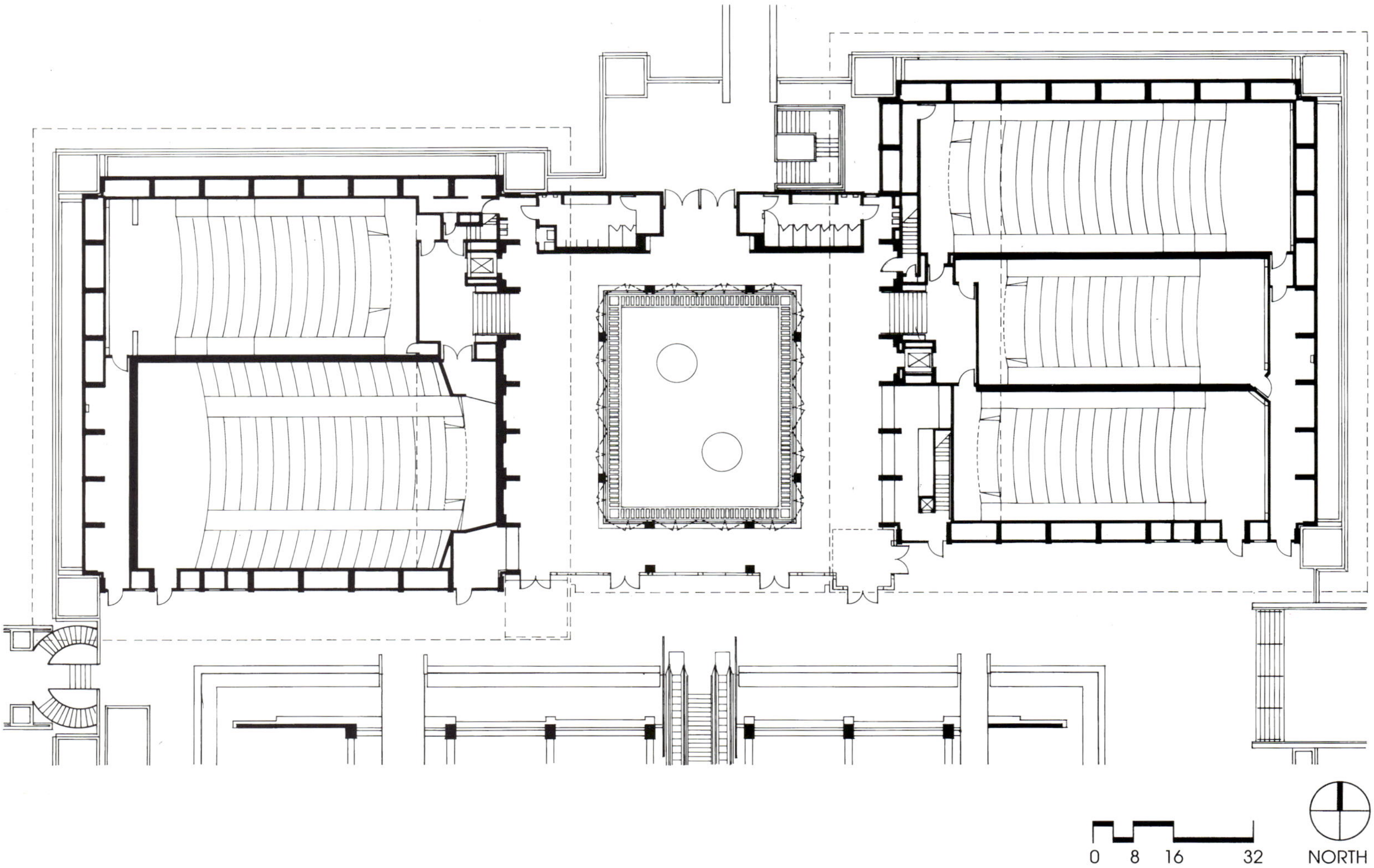

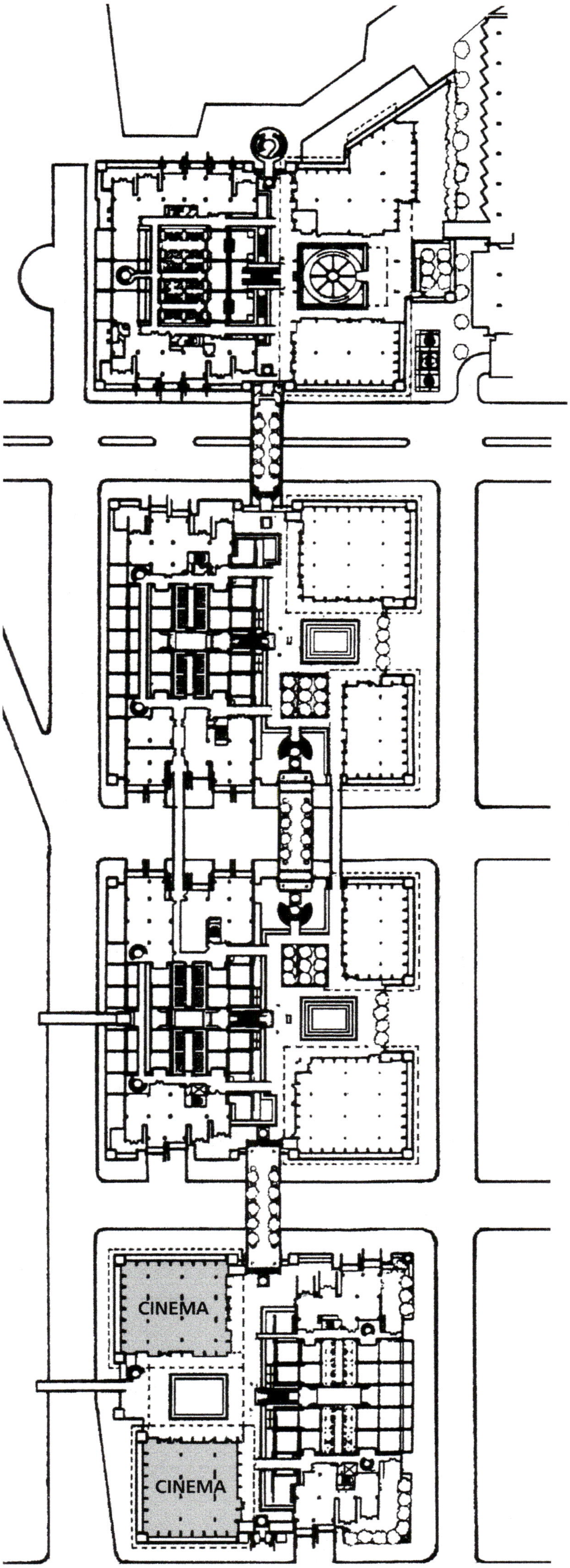

Left, four blocks of
Embarcadero Center
public space and retail
renovation.
Below, new openings,
railings and canopies
improve circulation and
visibility in the Center's
retail and public spaces.

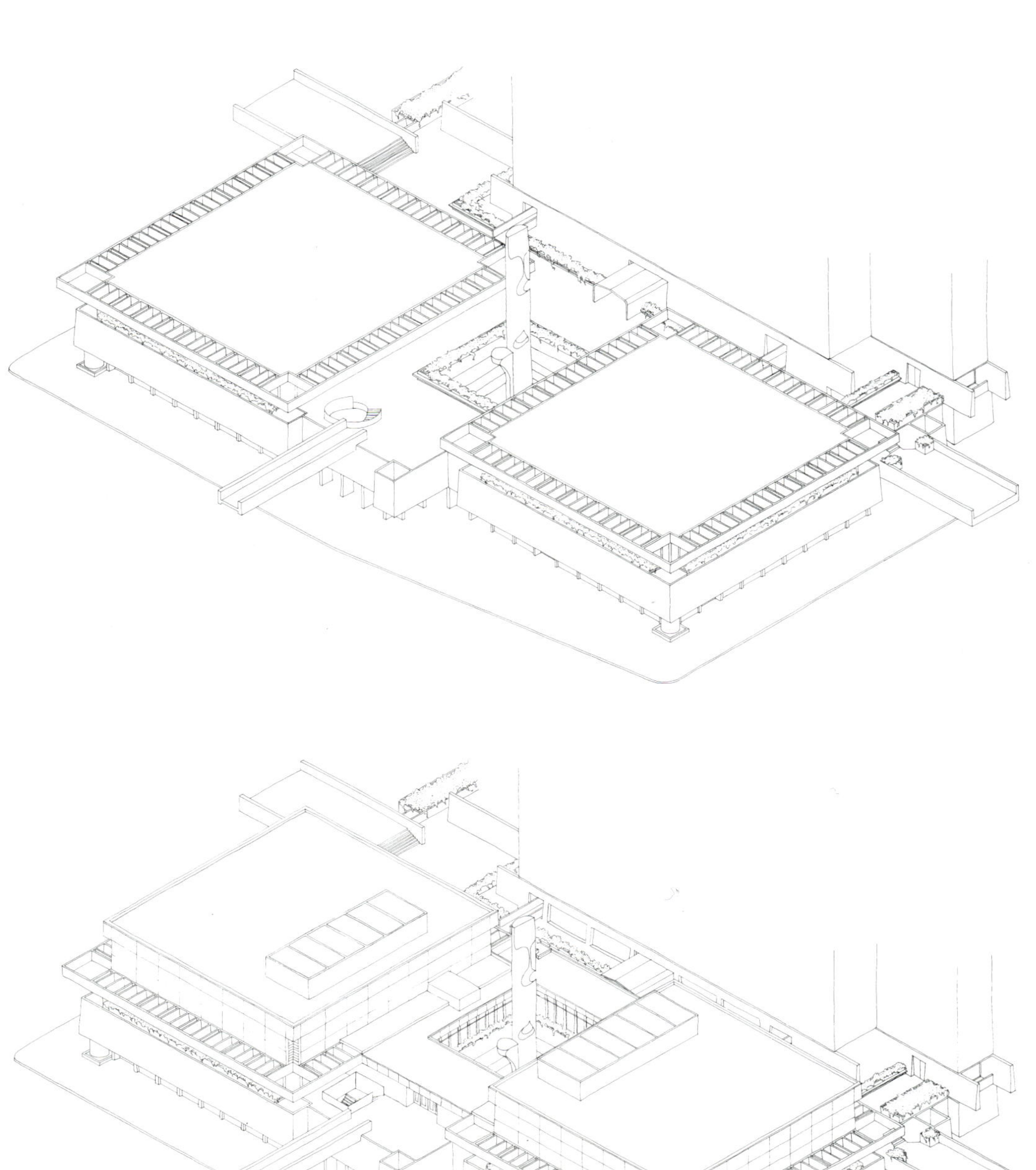


Axonometric of the
complex before (above)
and after (below) the
project.

The new cinema from
a pedestrian bridge.
Following pages,
nighttime view of
the complex showing
the shops at street level
and the movie theaters
above.

CINEMA
Battery
BATTERY
Front

EMBARCADERO CENTER
CINEMA
CINEMA

# Irvington Community Center

*Client*
City of Fremont

*Architects*
ELS/Elbasani & Logan Architects

*Engineers*
E.G. Hirsch & Associates (Structural)
MCT Engineers, Inc. (Mechanical/Electrical)

*Landscape Architect*
Stephanie McAllister Landscape Architect

*Lighting Consultant*
Becca Foster Lighting Design

*General Contractor*
W.A. Thomas Co., Inc.

*Photographer*
David Wakely

*Publications*
"l'Arca", No.112 February 1997
"Architectural Record", June 1996
"San Jose Mercury News", May 19, 1996

*Awards*
1996 National Association of Homebuilders
    Merit Award
1996 AIA, East Bay Chapter Citation
1996 AIA, California Council Merit Award

This new community center serves the Irvington neighborhood in suburban Fremont, California. The immediate context includes a high school, a church and its parking lot, and a continuation high school. With one entry on the street and another facing the existing park, the design reflects the building's dual civic and recreational functions.

A central lobby bisects the building, with a gymnasium on one side, and a community meeting room, a "tiny tots" room, and restrooms on the other. The cross section features a dramatic roof structure with skylights in the gymnasium, exposed steel framing and clerestory in the lobby, and high ceilings and skylights in the community rooms. On the exterior, to a height of eight feet above grade, flowering plants grow on stainless steel espaliers.

Vine-covered walls discourage graffiti and require little maintenance.

The entry lobby, bright and airy during the day, glows at night. It serves both as a circulation and meeting space for students from nearby schools.

"Barn" doors on the street and park sides can be opened to reveal gymnasium activities within.

Landscaping includes a plaza at the north entrance to the building, a mounded lawn area on the south end of the gym, and new walkways linking the building to the existing park and parking.

The community center draws citizens from all over Fremont and is a new source of civic pride for this suburban community.

Above, the west facade;
the complex is split into
two units around
a central lobby.
The various functions
are highlighted on
the outside by the use
of different materials.
Below, the gym entrance
clad with strips of wood
and wide openings.
Opposite page, site plan.

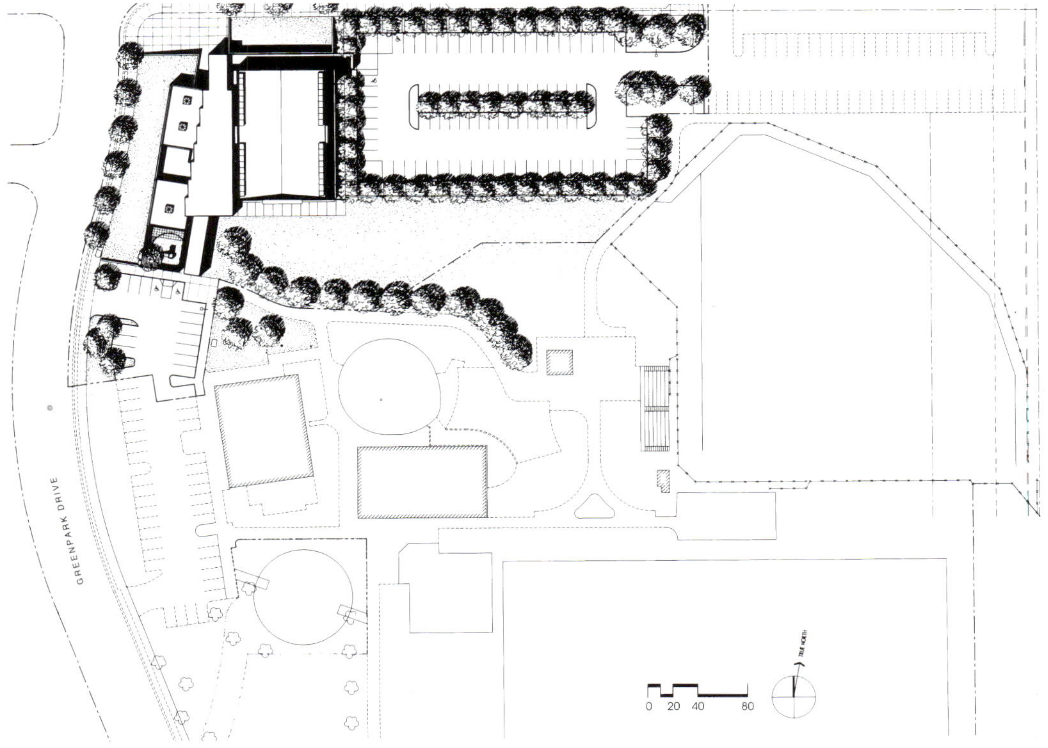


GREENPARK DRIVE
0  20  40      80

The information desk
in the lobby separating
the center's two main
buildings.

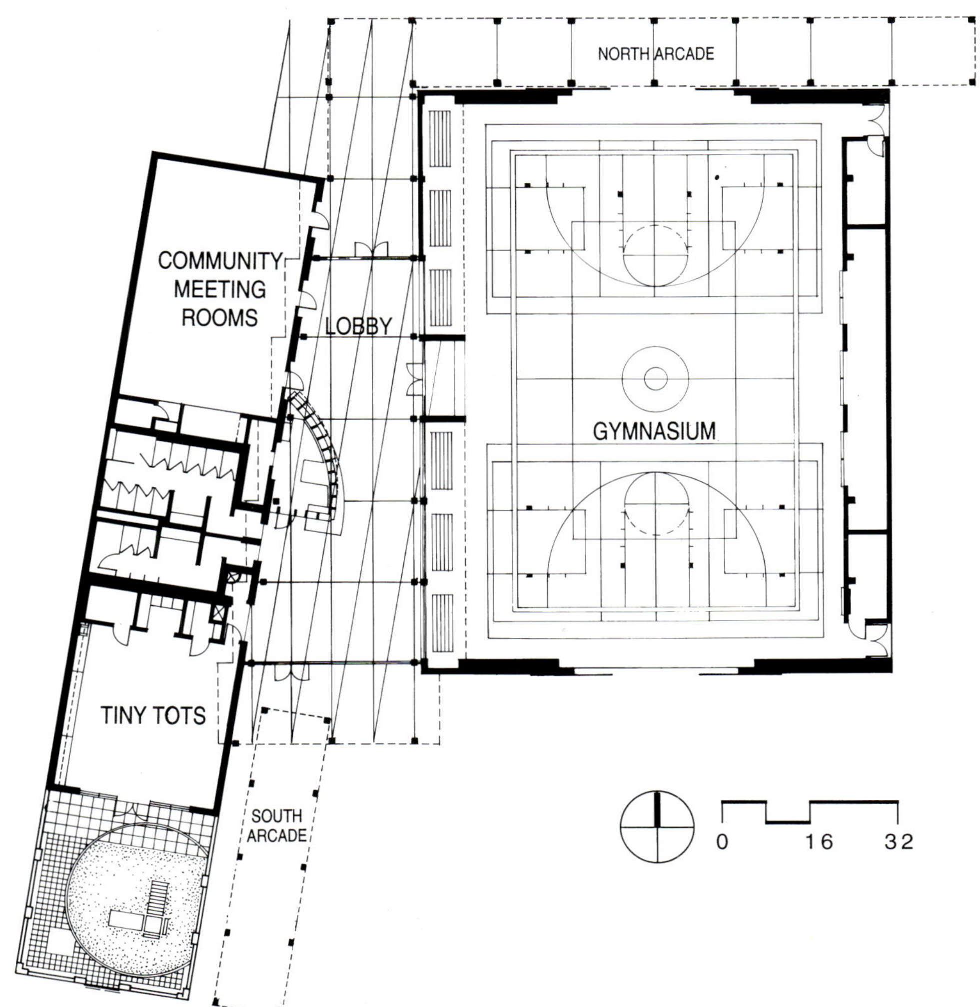

Above, the central lobby dictating the complex's spatial layout. The side facing the gym is made entirely of glass so that people can watch the sports activities. Right, ground-floor plan.

View from the inside of
the gym entrance.

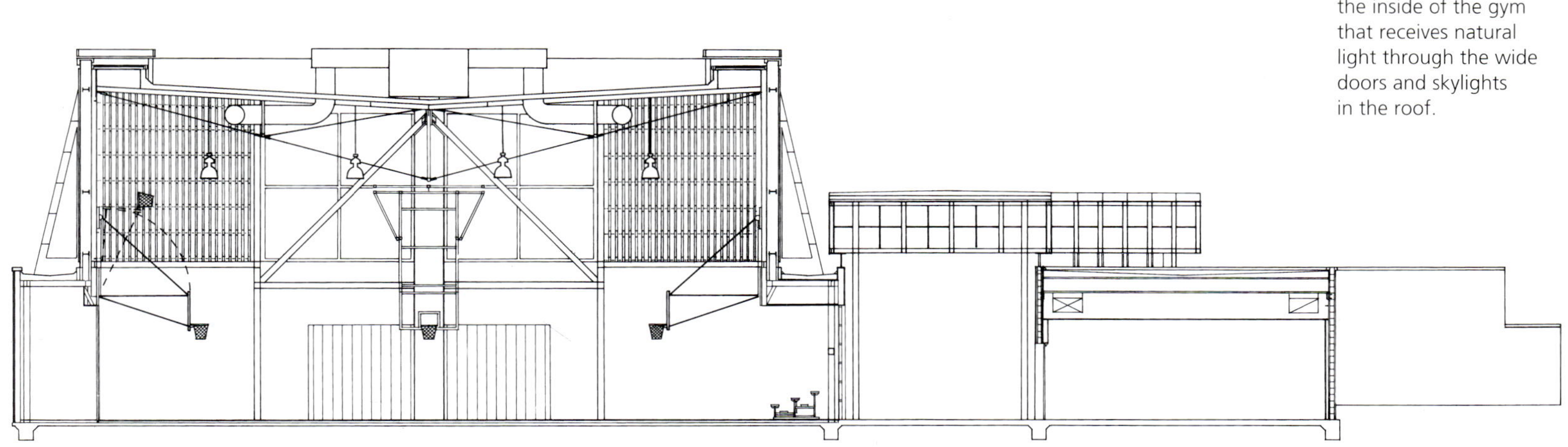

Cross section towards the south. Below, the inside of the gym that receives natural light through the wide doors and skylights in the roof.

Nighttime view of park
entrance to the Center.

# Denver Pavilions

*Client*
Denver Pavilions Limited Partnership

*Architects*
ELS/Elbasani & Logan Architects

*Engineer*
L.A. Fuess Partners Incorporated (Structural)

*Landscape Architects*
Civitas Inc.

*Graphics Consultant*
The Office of Reginald Wade Richey

*Lighting Consultant*
George Sexton Associates

*Acoustics Consultant*
Charles M. Salter Associates

The new Denver Pavilions, opening in late 1998, will fill two city blocks along downtown Denver's 16th  Street Mall.

The project reinforces the existing downtown fabric with a new retail concept. The Denver Pavilions will house high-profile national tenants, including Colorado's first Niketown, Virgin Records and Hard Rock Cafe and Wolfgang Puck Cafe, which will provide the draw needed to activate the project's outdoor public spaces and to revitalize the upper end of Denver's 16th  Street pedestrian mall. Mid block pedestrian streets were introduced to bring people into the project. A large curving wall exhibiting the project name unifies the two blocks and can be seen from afar.

Building elevations, massing and detailing take cues from nearby historic buildings without imitation. Within the urban district, the development assembles a dynamic mix of entertainment and dining venues, including two levels of restaurants and shops, several nightclubs above the third level, and a 15-screen cinema on the third and fourth levels. Underground parking will provide 800 spaces on two levels.

The destination project will become a retail and entertainment beacon for the entire Denver region.

DENVER

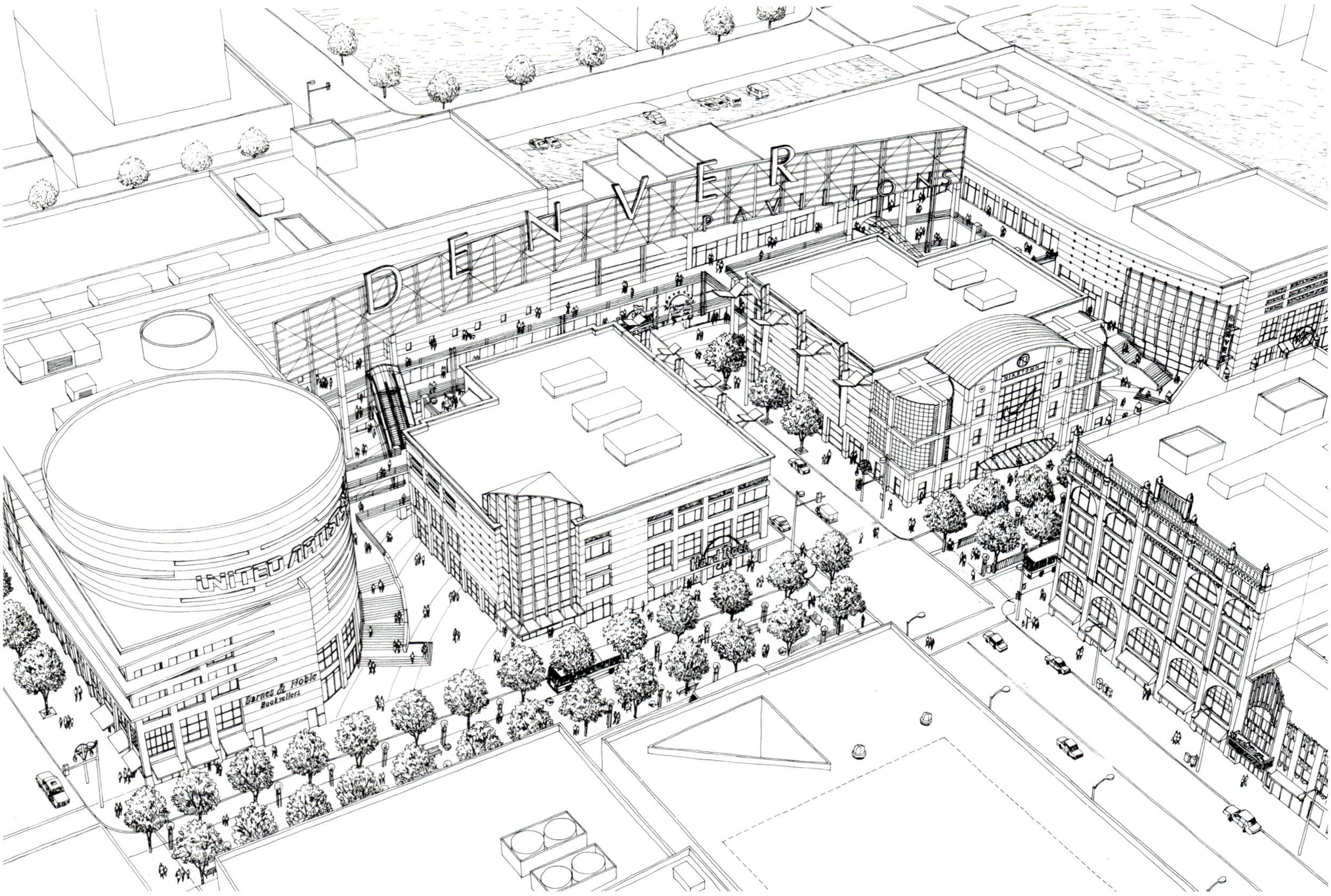

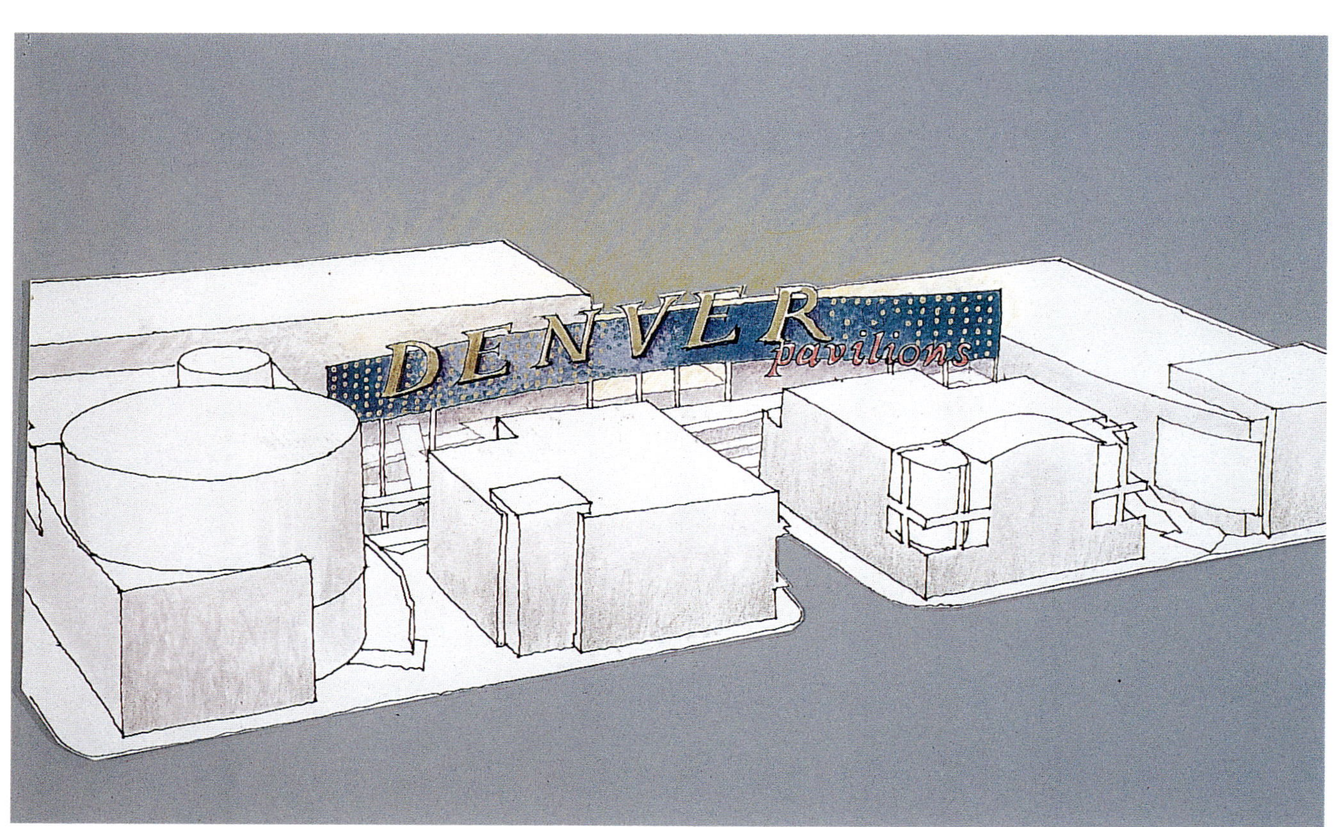

Above, bird's-eye view and, left, massing study. Opposite page, west elevation, east elevation and study for the paving pattern.

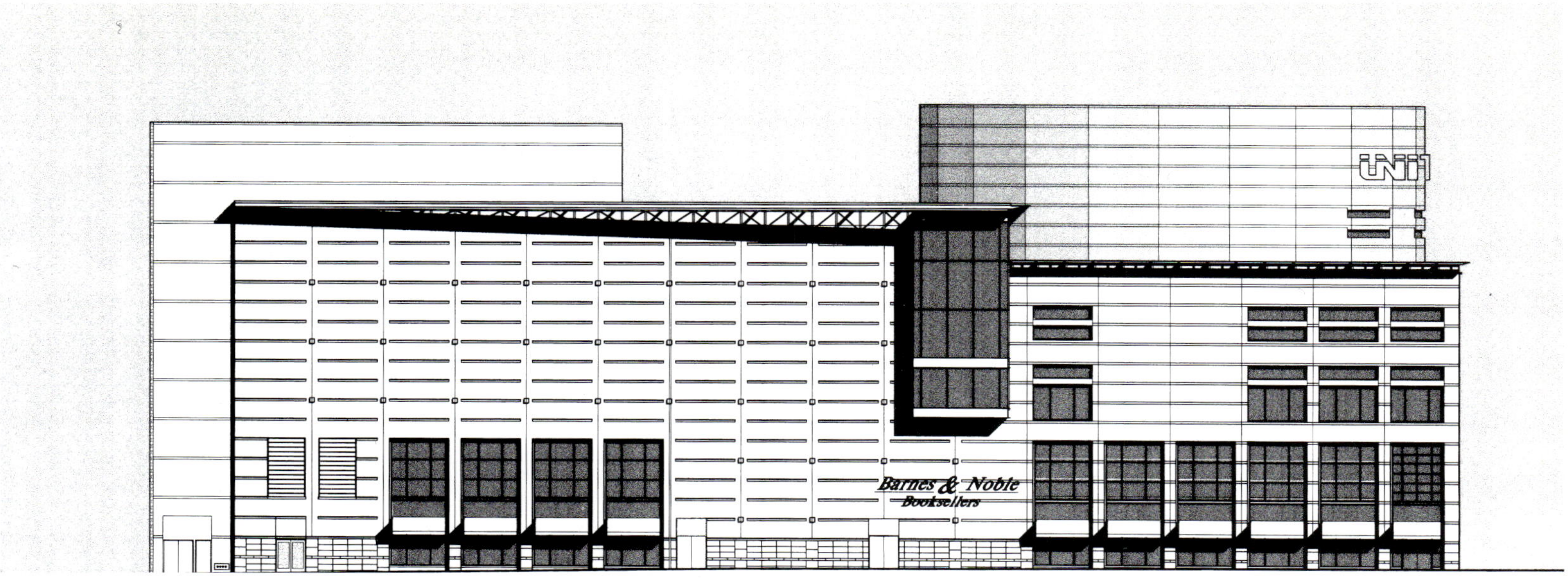

UNI
Barnes & Noble
Booksellers

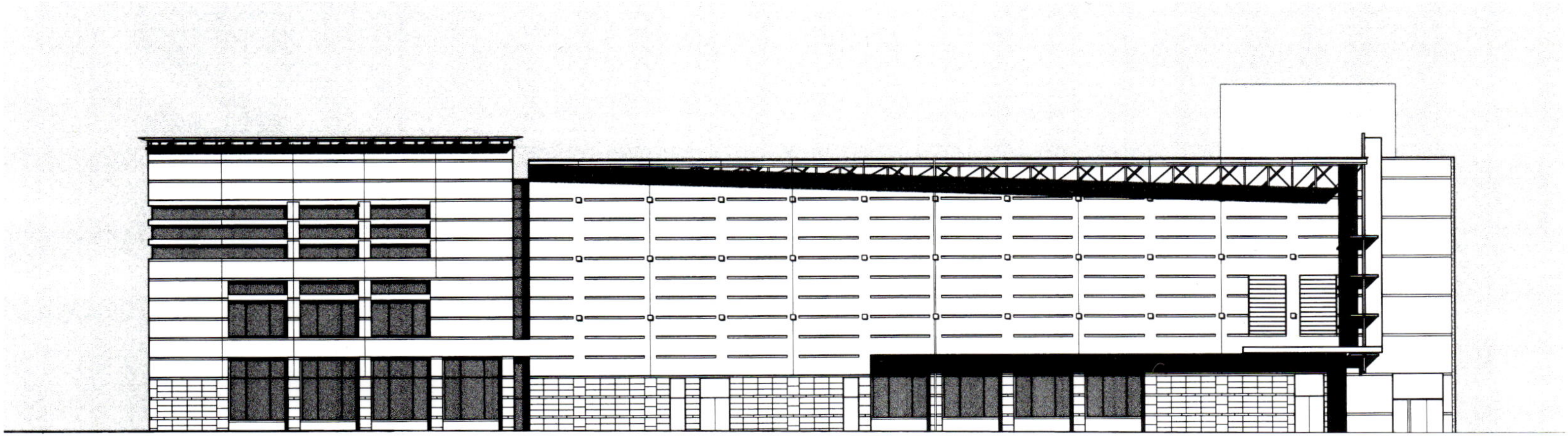

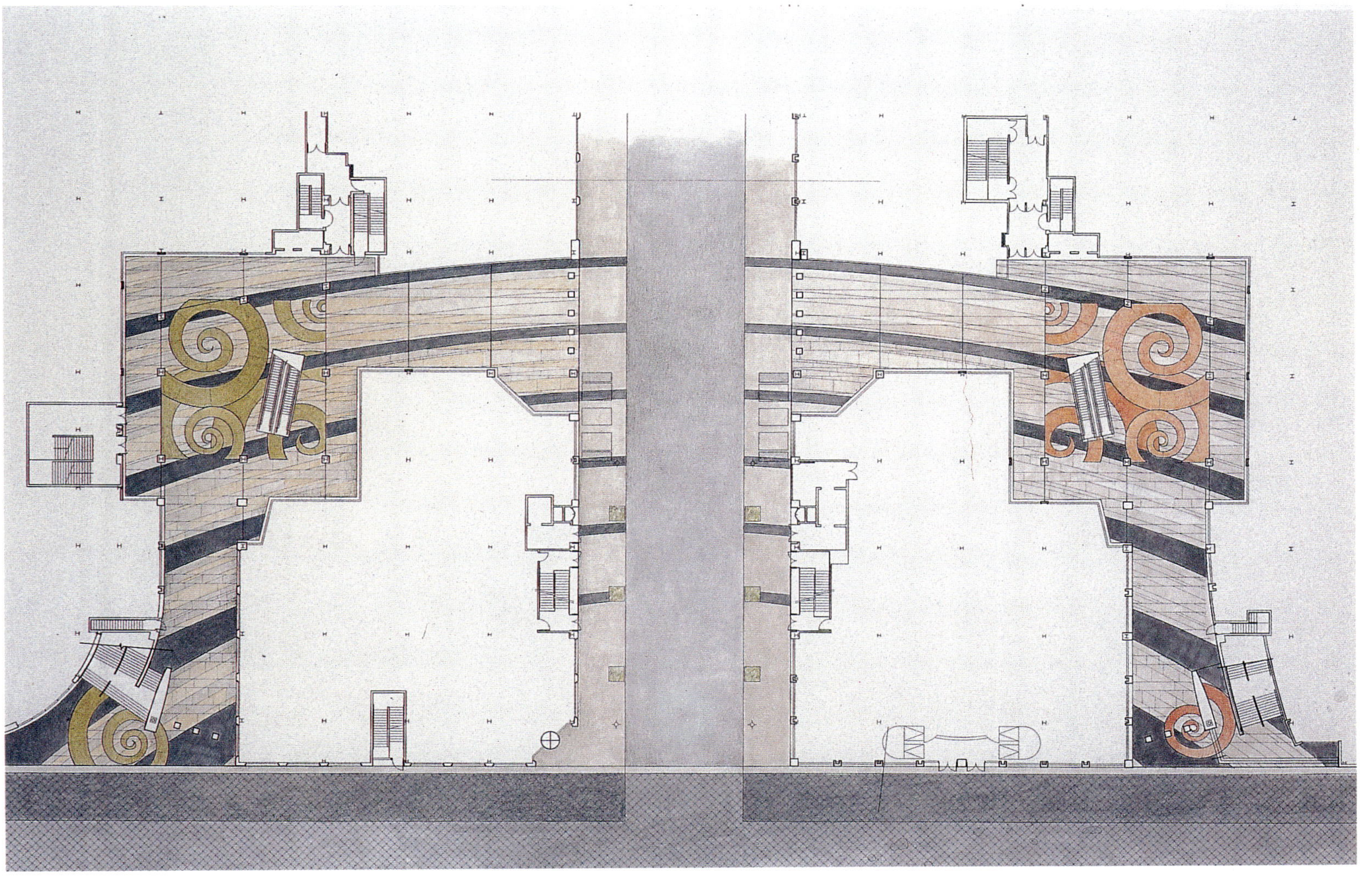

From bottom of page up, second-floor plan and third-floor plan. Opposite page, section showing sign detail.

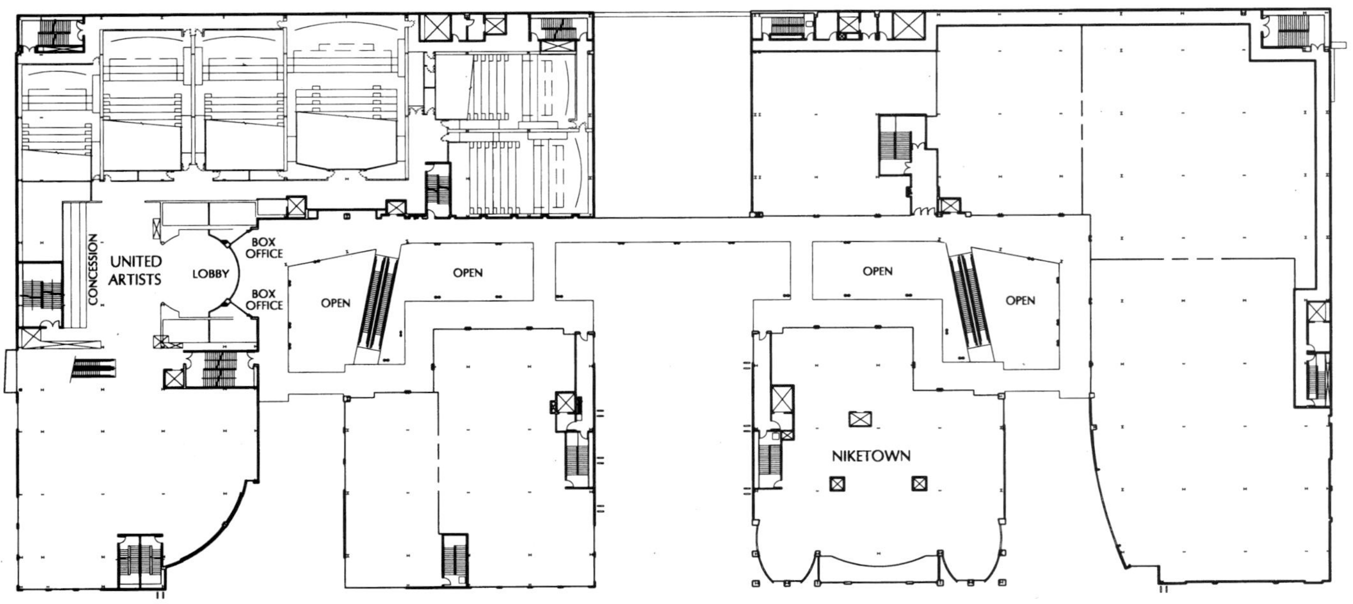

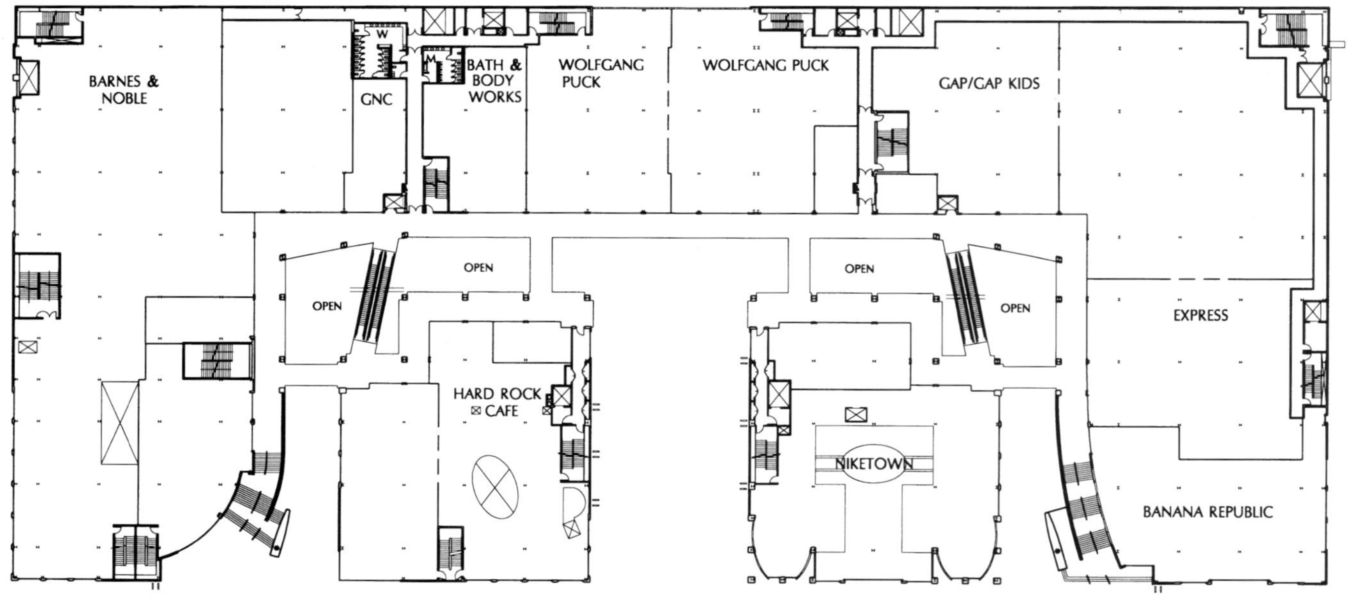

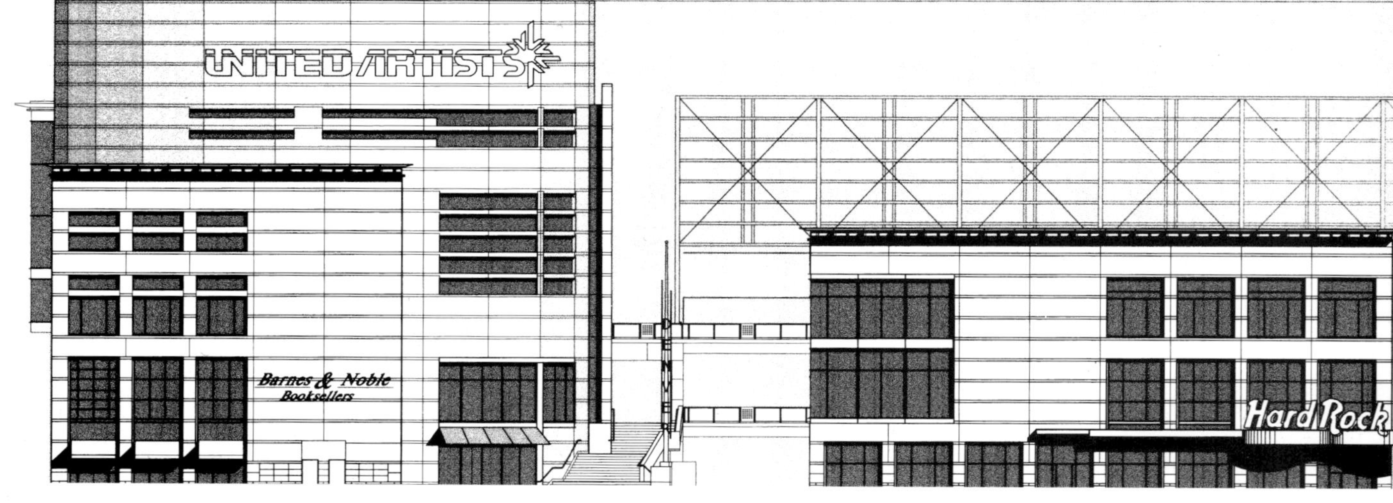

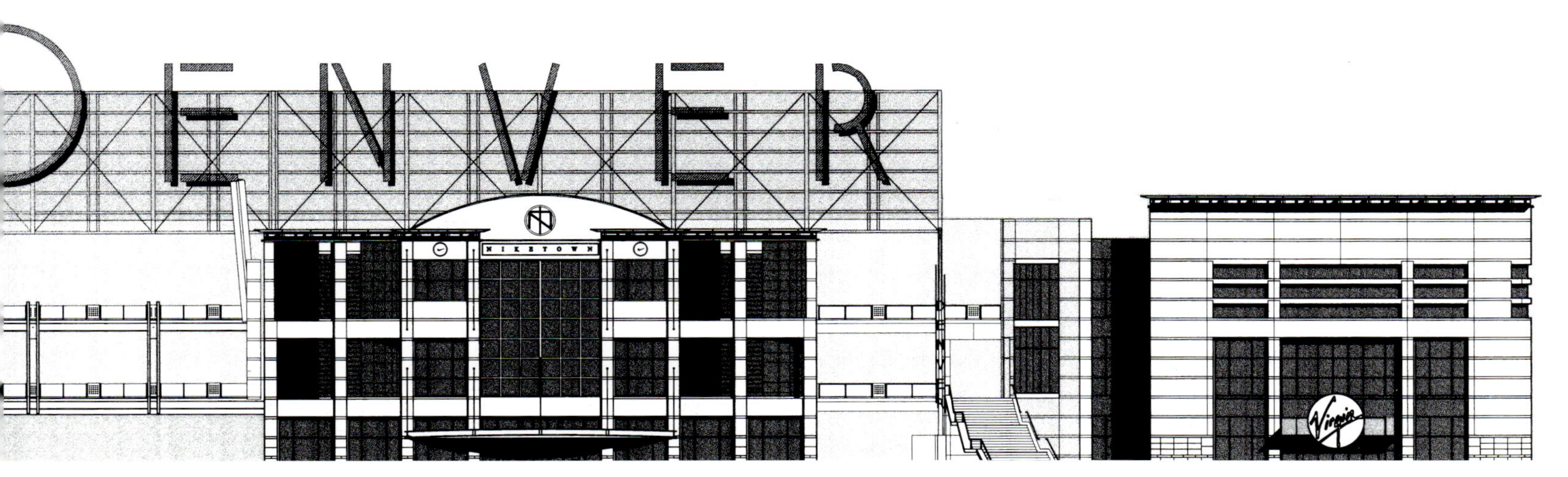


DENVER
Virgin

# Konak Pier Renovation

*Clients*
Cornerstone International
(Project Sponsor)

Izmer Inşaat Sanay Ticaret ve Turizm A.Ş.
(Project Developer)

*Design Architects*
ELS/Elbasani & Logan Architects

*Local Architect*
MATU Mimarlik, A.Ş.

*Master Plan*
EDAW, Inc./Christopher Degenhardt

*Structural Engineer*
Nu Inşaat Tesisat e Ticaret Ltd. Şti.

*Mechanical Engineer*
Eke Tesisat ve Ticaret A.Ş.

*Electrical Engineer*
Çağkor Elektrik Sanayi ve Ticaret Ltd. Şti.

Konak Pier contains a group of historic waterfront warehouses which were constructed in several phases between 1875 and 1890. The buildings will be restored, expanded, and converted to retail, dining and entertainment uses.

The Export Warehouse, designed by Gustav Eiffel and built in 1890, is Konak Pier's most important historic building. The structure was fabricated in Eiffel's workshop in Belgium, transported by ship, and constructed under the supervision of French engineers. Intricately detailed steel trusses sit on alternating cast iron columns and riveted plate steel columns, and continuous, peaked skylights light each bay.

Adjacent to Eiffel's building is the first warehouse constructed at Konak Pier, completed in 1876 (by unknown designers). The structural system consists of cast iron columns and steel trusses with a roof of Marseilles clay tiles resting on timber purlins. The exterior walls are plastered stone masonry with carved stone details. The French Customs Building, constructed between 1880-1883 of stone and wood, provides a classical façade to the warehouse on the main boulevard facing downtown Izmir's government and city core. For the past few decades, these structures were used for parking and housed maritime facilities.

Reuse and expansion plans adapt the structure to accommodate new uses and building systems without compromising the exposed structure and overall historic character. The new project program includes retail anchors, specialty shops, cafes, clubs, restaurants and cinemas. The specialty retail shops will take advantage of the high-volume, light-filled spaces in the Eiffel warehouses.

Fast food restaurants will be located on the new plaza along the south building edge. Overlooking Izmir Harbor and the planned future marina, restaurants and cafes will open onto the north Promenade edge of the pier.

CASABELLA
DIRECTORY

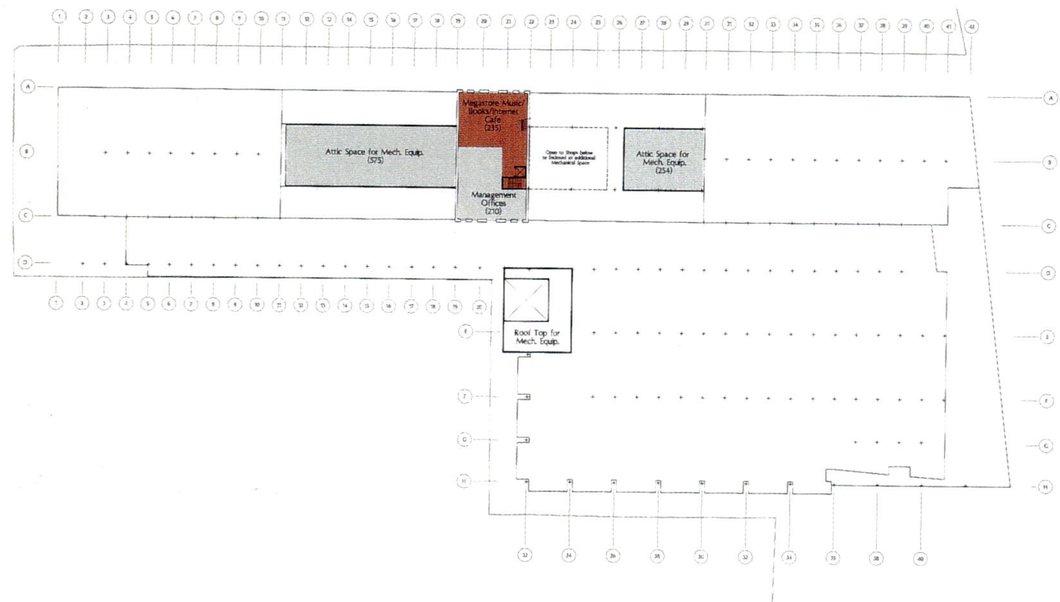

From bottom of page up, ground-floor plan, first-floor plan and second-floor plan. Below, north elevation.

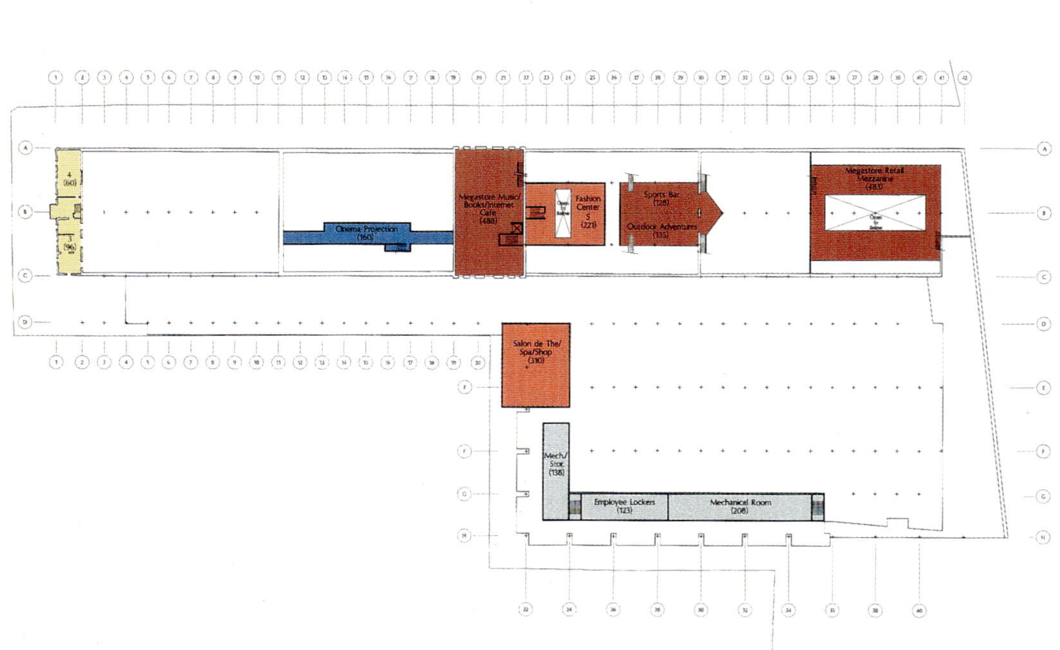

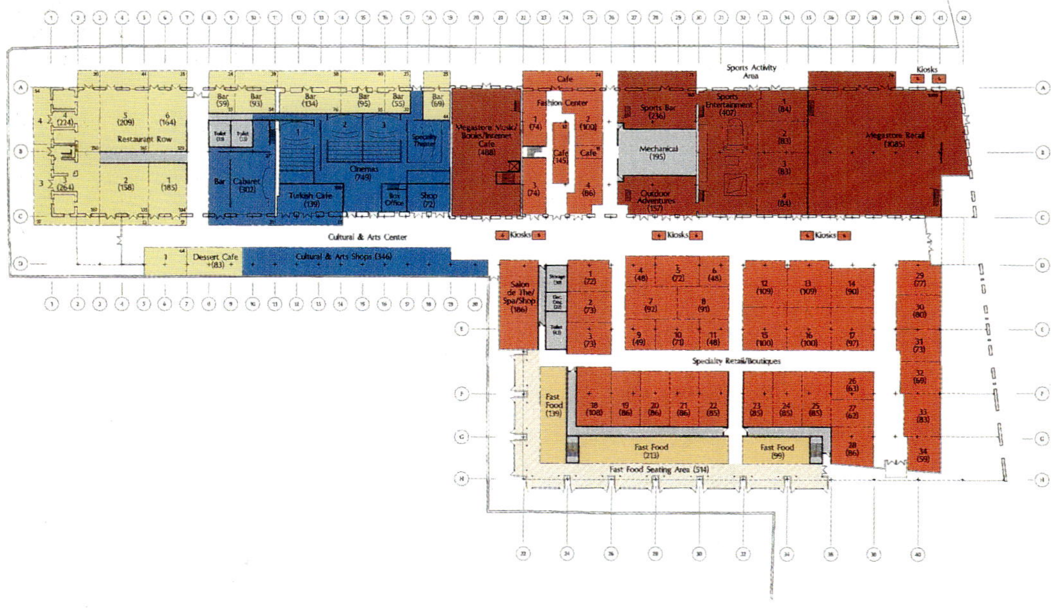

Right, pier before
renovation.

Above and below,
Konak Pier before
renovation.
Right, perspective view
of the project.

KONAK PIER

# List of Works

**1966**
Fremont Civic Center Competition
Fremont, California
*Second Prize*

**1967**
Birmingham Civic Center Competition
Birmingham, Alabama
*Finalist, Honorable Mention*

**1968**
Brighton Beach Housing Competition
Brooklyn, New York

International Headquarters Center
Vienna, Austria
*Honorable Mention*

**1969**
Thousand Oaks Civic Center Competition
Thousand Oaks, California
*Honorable Mention*

Yale Mathematics Building Competition
Yale University
New Haven, Connecticut

Trondheim New Town Competition
Trondheim, Norway

Side-Manavgat New Town Competition
Turkey

**1970**
Yonkers Urban Design Study
Yonkers, New York

**1971**
Matthaei Residence
Harbour Island, Bahamas

Place Beaubourg Competition
Paris, France

Getty Square Plaza
Yonkers, New York

**1973**
Broome County Arena
Binghamton, New York

World Savings Bank
Daly City, California

World Savings Bank
Salinas, California

**1974**
Georgetown Urban Development Plan
Georgetown, Washington D.C.

World Savings Bank
Moraga, California

Newark Airport Rapid Transit System
Newark International Airport
Newark, New Jersey

Niagara Falls Area A Design Study
Niagara Falls, New York

World Savings Bank Interior Design
Walnut Creek, California

**1975**
Transportation Action Kit
Plan for Public Policy Research Associates
& California State Assembly

The Foundry Historic Renovation
Georgetown, Washington D.C.

Exchange Place Mixed Use Center
Jersey City, New Jersey

Roosevelt Island Housing Competition
New York, New York
*First Prize*

Chinatown Redevelopment Mixed Use
Oakland, California

Nodine Terrace Housing
Yonkers, New York

**1976**
American Historical Truck Museum
Allentown, Pennsylvania

Aurora Civic Center Master Plan
Aurora, Illinois

Elkart Mixed Use Center Study
Elkart, Indiana

Riverfront Center Design Study
Flint, Michigan

Kalamazoo Conference Center & Hotel
Kalamazoo, Michigan

Toledo Downtown Planning & Feasibility Study
Toledo, Ohio

**1977**
University Avenue Co-op
Master Planning & Renovation
Berkeley, California

The Brewery Mixed Use Center Design
Milwaukee, Wisconsin

Monterey Hills Redevelopment Plan
Monterey Hills, California

Energy Efficient State Office Building
Competition
Sacramento, California
*Second Place*

**1978**
Monterey Hills Village Housing
Monterey Hills, California

**1979**
Paramount Arts Center
Aurora, Illinois

ELS Offices
Berkeley, California

Eugene Downtown Development Offering
Eugene, Oregon

Marks Residence
Honolulu, Hawaii

Campus Events Facility
University of California
Santa Barbara, California

**1980**
Allen Condominiums
Berkeley, California

Lawrence Berkeley Laboratory Master Plan
University of California
Berkeley, California

University Town Center Master Plan
Irvine, California

Phoenix Downtown Plan
Phoenix, Arizona

Long Range Development Plan,
U.S. Government Properties
Seoul, Korea

Lowertown, Block 40 Master Plan
St. Paul, Minnesota

**1981**
Troy Retail Center
Troy, New York

**1982**
Baltimore Inner Harbor Competition
Baltimore, Maryland

Evanston Concept Development Plan
Evanston, Illinois

Capitol Center
Madison, Wisconsin

The Grand Avenue
Milwaukee, Wisconsin

Morrison Street Plan
Portland, Oregon

La Entrada Master Plan
Tucson, Arizona

**1983**
University of California Press
Berkeley, California

Recreational Sports Facility
University of California
Berkeley, California

Embassy Staff Housing
Manila, Philippines

Oakland Convention Center
& Hyatt Regency Hotel
Oakland, California

Energy Efficient State Office Building
San Jose, California

**1984**
Highland Park Center
Denver, Colorado

Circle Center Design Competition
Indianapolis, Indiana

30th Street Train Station
Philadelphia, Pennsylvania

Arlene Schnitzer Concert Hall
Portland Center for Performing Arts
Portland, Oregon

**1985**
The Forum Mixed Use Center Design
Houston, Texas

Oakland Mixed Use Study
Oakland, California

Santa Ana Mixed Use Government Center
Design
Santa Ana, California

Santa Barbara Retail Center Competition
Santa Barbara, California

Fine Arts Competition
Arizona State University
Tempe, Arizona

**1986**
Glendale Downtown Urban Design Plan
Glendale, California

Oakland City Hall Plaza Competition
Oakland, California
*Third Prize*

Oceanside Civic Center Design Competition
Oceanside, California

Phoenix Civic Center Design Competition
Phoenix, Arizona

Adams & Monroe Street Urban Design
Phoenix, Arizona

Tempe Mission Palms Hotel & Conference
Center
Tempe, Arizona

Bekins Warehouse Building Renovation
Walnut Creek, California

**1987**
BART Joint Development Studies
Alameda & Contra Costa Counties, California

Concord Downtown Urban Design Plan
Concord, California

Corte Madera Village Square Plan
Corte Madera, California

Winningstad & Intermediate Theaters
Portland Center for Performing Arts
Portland, Oregon

Mission Bay Urban Design Plan
San Francisco, California

Pier 45 Design Competition
San Francisco, California

Stanford University Athletics Regions
Master Plan
Stanford University, California

**1988**
Town Center (Mosque, Theater, Library, Hotel)
Jubail, Saudi Arabia

Defense Language Institute - Student Housing
Presidio of Monterey, California

Crocker Galleria Renovation
San Francisco, California

**1989**
Riverfront Research Park Master Plan
Eugene, Oregon

Ala Moana Center Renovation
Honolulu, Hawaii

Plaza Eight Cinemas
Pittsburg, California

Fifth Street Corridor Study
San Francisco, California

Santa Rosa Core Area Plan
Santa Rosa, California

**1990**
Fairfield Center for Creative Arts
Fairfield, California

Kuala Lumpur Master Plan Competition
Kuala Lumpur, Malaysia

Vista Ridge Mall
Lewisville, Texas

The Shops at Arizona Center
Phoenix, Arizona

Pioneer Place Mixed Use Center
Portland, Oregon

The Mission Inn Restoration
Riverside, California

North Campus Neighborhood Study
San Diego, California

Ronald McDonald House
San Francisco, California

Ford Center & Burnham Pavilion Renovation
Stanford University, California

Odaiba Mixed Use Competition
Tokyo, Japan

**1991**
Anaheim Downtown Plan
Anaheim, California

Courtyard House
Berkeley, California

Fremont Swim/Gym
Fremont, California

Gold Key Center Renovation & Expansion
Las Vegas, Nevada

Hiller Highlands Housing Master Plan
Oakland, California

Rockridge BART Station Mixed Use Plan
Oakland, California

North Downtown Master Plan
San Jose, California

San Mateo County Museum Complex Study
San Mateo, California

Davis Street Corridor Urban Design Plan
San Leandro, California

Vision 2020 Waikiki Master Plan
Honolulu, Hawaii

**1992**
Berlin Spreebogen Competition
Berlin, Germany

Anaheim Community Center
Union Pacific Railroad Station Renovation
Anaheim, California

San Pablo Avenue Urban Design Plan
Emeryville, California

Glendale Downtown Plan
Glendale, California

Brand Boulevard Streetscape
Glendale, California

Downtown Transit Study
Houston, Texas

Long Beach Downtown
Strategy for Development
Long Beach, California

Center for AIDS Services
Oakland, California

Symphony Plaza Housing Competition
San Leandro, California

**1993**
North Point Mall
Alpharetta, Georgia

Berkeley Downtown Design Guidelines
Berkeley, California

Modesto Redevelopment Area Master Plan
Modesto, California

Oakland Downtown Revitalization Plan
Oakland, California

Olympus Oaks Master Plan
Roseville, California

Hyatt Regency Hotel Renovation
San Francisco, California

Clarke Quay Historic District
Singapore

Kakaako Makai Master Plan
Honolulu, Hawaii

Recreation & Events Center
California Polytechnic State University
San Luis Obispo, California

**1994**
Bellevue Retail/Entertainment Center Design
Bellevue, Washington

Brea Urban Design
Brea, California

Dallas Retail/Entertainment Center Design
Dallas, Texas

East Baybridge Mixed Use Center
Emeryville, California

Valley Center for Performing Arts
Holy Names College
Oakland, California

Orlando Retail/Entertainment Center Design
Orlando, Florida

Sunset Boulevard Retail
Disney/MGM Studios
Orlando, Florida

Randall Museum Theater
San Francisco, California

Yerba Buena Gardens
Retail/Entertainment Design
San Francisco, California

Sunnyvale Urban Design
Sunnyvale, California

The Woodlands Mall
The Woodlands, Texas

**1995**
East Lone Tree Specific Plan
Antioch, California

The Citadel Renovation
Colorado Springs, Colorado

Irvington Community Center
Fremont, California

University Town Center Design
Kent, Ohio

Belle Haven Community Design
Menlo Park, California

Orinda Town Center Plan
Orinda, California

Salem Center Renovation
Salem, Oregon

Embarcadero Center Renovation
San Francisco, California

Embarcadero Center Cinemas
San Francisco, California

Eastridge Mall Renovation
San Jose, California

Ohlone Chynoweth Transit Village
San Jose, California

Central Park Plaza
San Mateo, California

Tiong Bahru Plaza
Singapore

**1996**
Pruneyard Retail Center Renovation
Campbell, California

Bank of America Branch
Palo Alto, California

Jantzen Beach Retail Center Renovation
Portland, Oregon

Dubai International Airport
Commercial, Hotel & Retail Design
Dubai, United Arab Emirates

**1997**
College of Alameda Renovation
Alameda, California

Evanston Triangle Competition
Evanston, Illinois
*Selected Team*

Livermore Planning Study
Livermore, California

Pleasanton Community Center
Pleasanton, California

Stanford Shopping Center Renovation
Palo Alto, California

Stanford Tennis Stadium
Stanford University, California

Mission Bay Retail Design Study
San Francisco, California

**1998**
Berkeley High School Renovations & Additions
Berkeley, California

Cragmont Elementary School
Berkeley, California

Longfellow Arts & Technology Middle School
Berkeley, California

Berkeley Civic Center Renovation
Berkeley, California

Saks Fifth Avenue
Blackhawk, California

Bentley High School
Lafayette, California

Denver Pavilions
Denver, Colorado

Konak Pier Renovation
Izmir, Turkey

Saks Fifth Avenue
La Jolla, California

The Marketplace at Oviedo Crossing
Oviedo, Florida

Vincent Park
Richmond, California

San Jose State University Gateways
San Jose, California

Live Oak Community & Aquatic Center
Santa Cruz, California

Santa Cruz High School Theater
Santa Cruz, California

# People

**Founding Principals**
Barry Elbasani FAIA
Donn Logan FAIA

**Managing Principal**
Carol Shen FAIA

**Principals**
Frank L. Fuller FAIA
David Petta AIA
Bruce Bullman
Avery Taylor Moore
Kurt Schindler

**Associate Principals**
Raul Anziani
Clarence D. Mamuyac Jr. AIA
Dorek Jamie Rusin

**Senior Associates**
David Fawcett
Edward Noland

**Associates**
Laura Blake AIA
Anthony Grand
Geno Yun
Jeffrey Zieba

**Vice President
Finance & Administration**
Janette Marie Gross

**Vice President Planning**
Kerry O'Banion AICP

**ELS Public Relations
Project Coordinator
for this Volume**
Kenneth Caldwell

The following professionals worked at ELS during the period covered by this volume:

Carl Abruzzese
Alexander C. Achimore
Nancy Adelson
Lyn Alhorn
David Alpert
Newell Arnerich
Mary Austern
Emily Bachman
Timothy Bade
David Baker
Philip Banta
Nancy L. Bardach
Antonia J. Bava
Michael E. Beall
Gregory J. Beck
Michael Bernard
Richard Best
Pamela A. Bicket
Ellen Bildsten
S. Ross Bogen
Alan Burkett
Robert Calderwood
Eileen Capitolo
K. Daryl Carrington
C. Lynn Cary
Gonzalo Castro
Clifford L. Chang
Ling-Shen Chen
Pauline Chin
Thomas Chytrowski
Jeffrey M. Clark
Robyn Clark
Al Costa
Constance Curtis
Anthony Cutri
Rosa De La Sota
Gregg De Meza
Joe Decredico
Robert Diaz
Donna Dumont
George Duncan
John G. Ellis
Sirkku Fisher
Richard Forbes
Larry Fournier
Joshua Francis
Frank Frost
Miguel Fuentevilla
Daniel Garcia
Jose Garcia
Leslie B. Golden
Gregory Good
Amy Guiang
Clifford Ham
Thomas B. Harry
Cletus P. Hasslinger

Diana Hayton
Steven Heisler
Steven Hergert
John T. Hood
Norman Hooks
David Hruska
David Hurley
Andrew N. Jacobson
Gary M. Jereczek
Kelly Johnson
Marcy G. Jones
Wesley Jones
Sofia G. Jopillo
Christopher Jung
Eric Jung
Kazuko Kadogawa-Gill
Kenneth Kaji
Wayne Katsumata
Brenda Kennard
Joseph Kilanowski
Helen Kim
Young-Il Kim
Joseph King
Kenneth George Klumb
Lori Klumb
Klara Komorus-Towey
Tony K. Lam
Kenneth Law
Elaine Lee
John V.Y. Lee
Richard Lee
Scott Lentz
Robin Levitt
Wanda Liebermann
Yim Lim
Gary Logsdon
Kristin Low
William Allen Lowry Jr.
Larry B. Mack
Barbara Maloney
Peter Marciano
Anne Marshall
Patricia Maruya
Kenwood McQuade
Kathie S. Milano
Joel Mirogilo
Irene S. Mitsuhashi
Gregory Mockford
Ali R. Mogghadasi
Thomas Monahan
Mark Moreno
Cheryl Morgan
William J. Mudgett
Shireen Naghshineh
Gerald Navarro
Alan Ohashi
Terry J. Oksner
Roger K. Olpin
George Omura
Bonnie Ott

Mark Pearcy
Ellie Petrides
Karin L. Pfluger
Nicholas Phillips
Sharon L. Polledri
Bruce A. Race
Nancy Roberts
Greg Roja
Guillermo Rossello
Hector Rubio
David G. Sabalvaro
Jack S. Sagen
Ramon Santos
Gabrielle Saponara
John Sargent
T. Kevin Sayama
Anna Scheidegger
Katherine Schwertner
Jessica L. Seaton
Michael L. Severin
Bryan R. Shiles
Mark Smith
Pauline Souza
Daniel Stebbins
Richard Steele
Gregory Stewart
Alan D. Stiles
Jim Stone
Vincent Taboada Jr.
Paulett L. Taggart
Vandy S. Tam
Bruce Teel
Karen Tham
Mitchell Tobias
Harry Topping
Thomas J. Towey
Elizabeth Traugott-Browne
Robert S. Tsubamoto
Wendy Tsuji
Erin K. Uesugi
David M. Vala
Jose Vilar
Michele Vonk
Susan Weinraub
Daniel Wetherell
Manuel Wiesendanger
Steven R. Winkel
Matthew J. Winkelstein
Coulter Winn
Anton Wong
Howard Wong
Deborah Woodbury
Kenneth Y. Yamamoto
Jean C. Young
Colette Zee
Kenneth Zinns
John Zissovici

We regret any inaccuracies in this list.

Left to right  *Back Row:* Kurt Schindler, David Petta, Kerry O'Banion, D. Jamie Rusin, Frank L. Fuller,
Bruce Bullman, Raul Anziani, Geno Yun, Edward Noland
*Middle  Row:* Barry Elbasani, Laura Blake, Anthony Grand, Avery Taylor Moore, Donn Logan, Carol Shen
*Front Row:* Clarence D. Mamuyac, Jr., David Fawcett, Janette Marie Gross
*Not Pictured:* Jeffrey Zieba